AF880186

THE LOUISIANA CEMETERY FORMS BOOK

This book is a guide for interested notaries, attorneys, funeral directors, church officials, and cemetery directors. It is not legal advice nor the practice of law. The author draws on his practical experience in the field as a cemetery director and as a commissioned Louisiana Civil Law Notary Public, but does not hold himself out to be an attorney at law. Those using any suggestions and forms are advised to confirm and update them with their own research. Use of this book constitutes full and voluntary acceptance of the risk of error, misapplication, or invalidity.

Any statement of "should" or "is advised" or similar is based on the author's personal and practical experience. It is not legal advice.

THE LOUISIANA CEMETERY FORMS BOOK

Documents, Templates, and Compliance Tools for Cemetery Authorities and Notaries Public

A companion volume containing practical forms, sample contracts, affidavits, and checklists for daily operations.

JOSHUA R. LEBLANC

Bayou State
PUBLISHING

For permission requests, contact:
Bayou State Publications
P.O. Box 1049
Abbeville, LA 70511
Email: info@bayoustatepublications.com
Website: bayoustatepublications.com

ISBN: 978-1-970659-00-9

Printed in the United States of America
First Edition, 2025

Published by **Bayou State Publishing**
Youngsville, LA

Disclaimer:
The information contained in this book is provided for general educational and informational purposes only. Nothing in this book should be construed as, or relied upon as, legal advice. Laws and regulations vary by jurisdiction and are subject to change. Readers are strongly encouraged to consult with a qualified attorney before making any decisions or taking any action based on the material presented herein. The author and publisher expressly disclaim any liability for actions taken or not taken based on the contents of this book.

About the Author

Joshua R. LeBlanc serves as the Executive Director of Holy Family Cemetery in New Iberia, Louisiana. He was ordained a Catholic deacon for the Diocese of Lafayette in 2016 and is currently assigned to St. Martin de Tours Catholic Church in St. Martinville.

Deacon LeBlanc brings a unique combination of theological insight, pastoral care, and administrative precision to the sacred work of cemetery management.

He holds a Master of Arts in Moral Theology and a +30 in Bioethics from Holy Apostles College and Seminary and is certified in Bioethics by the National Catholic Bioethics Center. He is currently pursuing a Doctorate in the field of Bioethics.

In addition to his ministry and administrative leadership, Deacon LeBlanc is a commissioned Civil Law Notary Public in and for the State of Louisiana and the owner of two small businesses — an IT firm and Chesterton's Fine Cigars in Youngsville, La. It is through this background that he shares his expertise in faith, ethics, and cemetery law.

Deacon LeBlanc also serves as a police chaplain and reserve police officer for the Youngsville and Abbeville Police Departments. He is also chaplain for the Military and Hospitaller Order of St. Lazarus of Jerusalem in the rank of Ecclesiastical Commander, whose mission is to serve the sick and dying. He is the Delegate for the Imperial Calcasieu Delegation and Vice Chancellor for Communications for the Grand Priory of America

As a deacon, he has ministered to grieving families for years, guiding them through the Catholic Church's teachings on death, burial, and resurrection. As a professional cemetery administrator, he has developed robust compliance systems rooted in Louisiana law, ensuring that every interment, fund, and record upholds both the dignity of the deceased and the legal obligations of the living.

Deacon LeBlanc is the author of *The Louisiana Cemetery Handbook: Laws, Compliance, and Administration*, A comprehensive guide to Louisiana cemetery law, Title 8 statutes, case law, and regulatory compliance.. Together, these works form the foundation of *The Louisiana Cemetery Authority Series*, a comprehensive legal and operational reference for religious and civil cemetery professionals throughout the state.

He and his wife, Annie, reside in Abbeville, Louisiana, with their cat Benedict.

THE LOUISIANA CEMETERY AUTHORITY SERIES

The Louisiana Cemetery Handbook: Law, Compliance, and Administration: A comprehensive guide to Louisiana cemetery law, Title 8 statutes, case law, and regulatory compliance.

The Louisiana Cemetery Forms Book: Documents, Templates, and Compliance Tools for Cemetery Authorities and Notaries Public. A companion volume containing practical forms, sample contracts, affidavits, and checklists for daily operations.

Catholic and Cultural Burial Traditions in Louisiana: A Guide to Faith, Heritage, and Sacred Practice. A comprehensive exploration of Louisiana's Catholic, Cajun, Creole, African American, and Native burial customs, offering theological insight, cultural history, and practical guidance for cemetery professionals and families.

Louisiana Cemetery Case Law: Jurisprudence, Practical Lessons, and Title 8 in the Courts. A clear and practical guide to Louisiana's major cemetery cases, this volume explains how courts interpret Title 8 in real-world disputes involving burial authority, disinterment, family cemeteries, undeveloped land sales, trust funds, and historic burial protections.

The Notary's Guide to Louisiana Cemetery Law: Authority, Documentation, and Practice Under Title 8. A practical reference that equips Louisiana notaries with clear, compliant language, clauses, and pastoral guidance for navigating cemetery ownership, interment rights, and Title 8 obligations in everyday notarial practice.

NOTICE OF USE AND COPYRIGHT RESTRICTIONS

THE FIRST BOOK IN THIS SERIES

THE LOUISIANA CEMETERY HANDBOOK

Law, Compliance, and Administration

The *Louisiana Cemetery Handbook* is the state's most comprehensive and authoritative guide to the legal, historical, and operational foundations of cemetery management in Louisiana. Written for cemetery authorities, notaries public, attorneys, clergy, and municipal officials, it explains—in clear and practical language—**how Louisiana's unique burial laws work** and how they should be applied in everyday cemetery operations.

Now available through participating bookstores and online at Amazon.com.

This essential volume includes:

- **A full explanation of Louisiana's cemetery laws**, including Title 8, Louisiana Civil Code, and relevant Administrative Code provisions.
- **Historical and cultural background** that illuminates why Louisiana's cemetery laws are distinct from those of any other state.
- **Detailed commentary on interment rights, perpetual care, abandonment procedures, dedication and removal, disinterment, merchandise trust laws, succession issues, and more.**
- **Best-practice guidelines** for cemetery operations, recordkeeping, trust fund compliance, and consumer protection.
- **Practical examples, case studies, and diagrams** to help cemetery personnel apply the law correctly.
- **Professional insights** informed by the author's experience in cemetery administration, notarial practice, and pastoral ministry.

WHY THE HANDBOOK STANDS ALONE

While the Forms Book provides the tools, the *Louisiana Cemetery Handbook* provides the **knowledge, reasoning, and legal framework** behind those tools. It is the foundational reference every cemetery professional should have at their desk.

WHY YOU NEED BOTH VOLUMES

The Handbook and the Forms Book work together to create a complete, practical library:

- **The Handbook explains the law**, including its purpose, structure, and application.
- **The Forms Book puts the law into action**, offering compliant templates, affidavits, contracts, and checklists that flow directly from the principles explained in the Handbook.

Together, they ensure that **every interment, sale, transfer, and administrative act is handled lawfully, ethically, and efficiently**, reflecting both the letter of Louisiana law and the dignity owed to every family served.

TABLE OF CONTENTS

FRONT MATTER

PART I — ADMINISTRATION AND FOUNDATIONAL FORMS

PART II — INTERMENT RIGHTS AND SALES

PART III — INTERMENT AND DISINTERMENT

PART IV — PERPETUAL CARE AND TRUST FUNDS

PART V — ABANDONED SPACES AND REMOVAL OF DEDICATION

PART VI — NOTARIAL AND MISCELLANEOUS FORMS

PREFACE

Cemeteries hold not only the remains of those who have gone before us, but also the sacred trust of the living. That trust requires faithful stewardship, sound recordkeeping, and compliance with the civil and canonical laws that govern the care of the dead and the places of their repose.

The Louisiana Cemetery Forms Book has been prepared as the practical companion to *The Louisiana Cemetery Handbook: Law, Compliance, and Administration.* While the *Handbook* explains the "why" of cemetery law, this *Forms Book* provides the "how." It offers ready-to-use templates, affidavits, authorizations, contracts, and checklists designed to bring statutory and regulatory requirements into daily operational practice.

The forms contained herein are tailored specifically to the provisions of the **Louisiana Revised Statutes, Title 8 (Cemeteries)**, with attention to the decisions of Louisiana courts that have clarified the responsibilities of cemetery authorities. Where appropriate, forms reference related cases such as *Westlawn Cemeteries, Inc. v. Louisiana Cemetery Board* and *Sonnier v. Foundation of the Diocese of Lafayette, Inc.*, which have guided the interpretation of cemetery trust and interment laws.

This collection is offered as a resource for cemetery boards, religious corporations, funeral directors, notaries public, and all who share the sacred responsibility of ensuring that burial and memorialization are conducted with dignity, legality, and transparency. May this work assist those entrusted with the ministry of burial in preserving both the memory of the faithful departed and the integrity of those who serve them.

Joshua R. LeBlanc

INTRODUCTION

Cemetery management in Louisiana operates within a unique intersection of civil law, property law, trust law, and religious obligation. Title 8 of the *Louisiana Revised Statutes* establishes a comprehensive legal framework governing every aspect of cemetery operation—from perpetual care funds and merchandise trusts to disinterment, recordkeeping, and the removal of dedication.

In practice, however, compliance depends not only on knowledge of the law but on the consistent use of **properly drafted legal instruments**. Each burial authorization, affidavit, or board resolution serves as both an administrative record and a legal safeguard. Without transparent and standardized documentation, even well-intentioned cemetery authorities risk noncompliance with statutory requirements or the invalidation of transactions affecting interment rights.

This volume was developed to meet that need. Every form has been written in plain, professional language and formatted to comply with Louisiana notarial and recording standards. The collection includes:

- **Operational forms** for interment, disinterment, and recordkeeping.
- **Financial forms** for perpetual care and merchandise trust management.
- **Consumer protection forms** ensuring compliance with Title 8 sales and disclosure provisions.
- **Notarial and affidavit templates** suitable for use by Louisiana notaries public.
- **Administrative resolutions and checklists** for internal compliance and board governance.

Each form includes a statutory CITATION or legal reference, ensuring that users can easily verify the authority and purpose of each document within Louisiana law. The collection is organized into practical sections to reflect the daily workflow of a cemetery office.

While every effort has been made to ensure accuracy and completeness, this book should not be used as **a substitute for professional legal counsel**. Cemetery authorities should always seek guidance from an attorney or the **Louisiana Cemetery Board** when interpreting or applying the statutes to specific circumstances.

INSTRUCTIONS FOR USE

This volume is designed to serve both as a **working reference** and as a **legal template library** for Cemetery Authorities, boards of directors, notaries public, and funeral professionals in the State of Louisiana.

STRUCTURE AND ORGANIZATION

Forms are grouped according to subject matter—beginning with foundational and administrative documents and progressing through interment rights, perpetual care, disinterment, and consumer protection. Each part includes forms, affidavits, sample resolutions, and relevant statutory references.

Use the **Table of Contents** and **Index of Forms by CITATION** in the appendices to locate the desired form.

COMPLETING THE FORMS

- All forms are designed for **customization.** Fill in the blanks legibly or digitally with the appropriate names, dates, and locations.
- When required, select options in parentheses or check the checkboxes.
- Maintain consistent terminology with *Title 8* definitions – e.g., "interment rights" rather than "ownership of grave space."
- When a form includes a statutory reference (for example, **La. R.S. 8:659**), ensure the circumstances of its use meet that statute's requirements.

NOTARIAL USE

Many forms include Louisiana-specific **notarial acknowledgment blocks**, using the standard "State of Louisiana, Parish of ___" format. Any commissioned Louisiana Notary Public may execute these within jurisdictional limits. Forms that do not have Notarial information do not require notarization. Each form also explains the requirements for notarization specific to that form.

- Use the acknowledgment appropriate to the signer (individual, corporate officer, or religious authority).
- Where multiple signatures are required (for example, heirs or next of kin), each signer must appear before the notary unless otherwise provided by law.

Record-Keeping

Retain executed forms permanently as part of the **cemetery's perpetual record**, whether in paper or electronic format. Louisiana law requires cemetery authorities to preserve burial and ownership records indefinitely.

All transactions involving perpetual care or merchandise funds should be recorded in both the **cemetery ledger** and the **annual report** to the Louisiana Cemetery Board if required.

Customization and Adaptation

This collection provides **model forms** that users should adapt to their cemetery's unique policies, denominational customs, or corporate structure. Where necessary, forms may be re-typed on letterhead or incorporated into computerized cemetery management systems. Electronic versions of these forms are available by providing proof of purchase of this book at LaCemeteryBook.com.

Legal Consultation

Because Title 8 interacts with property, trust, and succession law, users should consult an attorney when questions arise concerning ownership disputes, abandonment, or disinterment. This volume is intended as a practical guide—not a source of legal advice.

Series Continuity

This book is Volume II of the *Louisiana Cemetery Authority Series.* Volume I, *The Louisiana Cemetery Handbook*, provides legal analysis, case law, and statutory interpretation that underpin these forms. Together, the two volumes form a complete legal and operational library for Louisiana cemetery management.

An editable Word version of each form is available for purchasers of this book. Contact the author using the contact form at LACemeteryBook.com

LOUISIANA CEMETERY FORMS FORMALITY MATRIX

I. GENERAL PRINCIPLES

Type of Transaction	Requires Authentic Form?	Reason
Cemetery ↔ Purchaser	❌ No	Covered by **La, R.S. 8:812(A)**; written signature sufficient.
Private ↔ Private Transfer	❌ No	**La. C.C. art. 1839** allows transactions to be passed by by Authentic Act or under private signature.
Donation / Dation / Partition	✅ Yes	Governed by **La. C.C. arts. 1536, 2655, 807.**

II. FORMS THAT MUST BE IN AUTHENTIC FORM

(Require execution before a notary and two witnesses; signed by all parties and notary.)

Form Title / Description	Reason / Authority	Citation(s)
Act of Donation of Interment Rights	Donations *inter vivos* of immovable property require authentic form under the Civil Code.	**La. C.C. art. 1536; La. R.S. 8:1(22)**
Dation en Paiement for Burial Space	Conveyance of immovable in satisfaction of a debt; must be authentic.	**La. C.C. art. 2655**
Burial Space Designation Trust (*inter vivos* trust instrument)	Trust instrument; must be in authentic or acknowledged form — authentic form preferred for recordation and clarity.	**La. R.S. 9:1752; La. R.S. 8:804**
Waiver of Interment Rights	Affects title or right to interment; must be authentic form as individuals do not usually give away things to which they are entitled.	**La. C.C art. 1541**
Declaration of Burial Rights or Family Interment Designation (when establishing ownership)	Determines interment rights in immovable property; an authentic act ensures enforceability after the owner's death.	**La. R.S. 8:803 – 804**
Partition or Reallocation of Family Burial Spaces	Division of real rights among heirs or co-owners; an authentic act is required.	**La. C.C. art. 807**

Form Title / Description	Reason / Authority	Citation(s)
Donation or Bequest Clauses in Wills naming burial spaces	Testamentary donation of immovable; must comply with testamentary authentic-form requirements.	**La. C.C. art. 1577**

III. FORMS THAT MAY BE IN ACKNOWLEDGED OR PRIVATE FORM

(Require signature and notarization, but not witnesses or full authentic form; acknowledgment before a notary is sufficient for acknowledgment and not required for private signature)

Form Title / Description	Reason / Authority	Citation(s)
Act of Sale or Transfer of Interment Rights Between Private Parties (not involving Cemetery Authority)	Private conveyance of immovable right; **La. CC. art. 2440** permits this to be done as acknowledgment or by private signature.	**La. C.C. art. 2440;**
Interment Right Purchase Agreement / Contract	Title 8 allows this to be done under private signature, but once signed by both parties, it has the character of an Authentic Act.	**La. R.S. 8:812**
Purchaser's Right of Cancellation Notice	Statutory notice, not conveyance of right; private signature sufficient.	**La. R.S. 8:802(F)**
Cancellation and Refund Request Form	Administrative action; private signature sufficient.	**La. R.S. 8:802(F); LAC 46:XIII.909(C)**
Affidavit of Heirship (Cemetery Space)	Factual affidavit; acknowledgment sufficient.	**La. C.C. art. 1836**
Correction of Errors by Cemetery Authority	Administrative correction; private signature sufficient.	**La. R.S. 35:2.1; La. R.S. 8:812**
Cemetery Permit / Work Order for Contractors	Operational authorization; not a property conveyance.	Not governed by the authentic act law
Perpetual Care Fund Deposit Form	Routine trust deposit report; private signature sufficient.	**LAC 46:XIII.909(C)**
Monthly Perpetual Care Reporting Form	Regulatory filing, no notarization required.	**LAC 46:XIII.909(C)**
Affidavit of Cancellation or Refund	Administrative acknowledgment; not a conveyance. Must be acknowledged.	**La. R.S. 8:802(F)**
Declaration Selecting Burial Location Among Owned Spaces	Internal family direction; not property transfer. Private signature sufficient.	**La. R.S. 8:804**
Cemetery Space Consignment Agreement	Contractual agreement; private signature sufficient.	**La. R.S. 8:812**
Cemetery Space Transfer Agreement (Authority-mediated)	Transfer through the Cemetery Authority; private signature is sufficient	**La. R.S. 8:812**

Form Title / Description	Reason / Authority	Citation(s)
Work Authorization or Monument Installation Form	Permission form; not a conveyance.	Administrative
Affidavit of Plaque Violation Notice or Removal	Factual notice; acknowledgment required.	Administrative

IV. GRAY-AREA FORMS

(Authentic form is recommended but not mandatory)

Form Title / Description	Rationale	Citation(s)
Burial Space Designation or Family Declaration (unrecorded)	Not strictly required, but authentic form provides evidentiary weight in disputes. Only private signature is legally required when done on the Cemetery Form. Acknowledgment is recommended.	**La. R.S. 8:804; La. C.C. art. 1836**
Reinterment Authorization / Disinterment Consent	Acknowledgment is sufficient, but authentic form is prudent to avoid challenge.	**La. R.S. 8:659–660**
Burial Space Family Trust Amendment	Amendment to trust; either authentic or acknowledged form allowed.	**La. R.S. 9:1752**
Notice of Abandonment or Declaration of Abandoned Space	Not strictly required by law to be authentic, but recordation is often sought.	**La. R.S. 8:308–310**

V. SUMMARY OF RULES

Category	Formality Required	Authority
Title 8: Conveyances by Cemetery Authority	Writing only (authentic form not required, but qualifies as an Authentic Act when signed by both parties.	**La. R.S. 8:812**
Private donations or conveyances of interment rights	🖋 Authentic Form Required	**La. C.C. art. 1536; 2440**
Administrative/regulatory forms	Acknowledgment or private signature	**LAC 46:XIII.909(C)**
Trust instruments	Authentic or acknowledged	**La. R.S. 9:1752**
Affidavits of fact	Acknowledged	**La. C.C. art. 1836**

VI. REQUIREMENTS BY FORM NUMBER

- 🖋 **AUTHENTIC ACT:** Must be executed before a notary public and two competent witnesses.
- 🖊 **NOTARIZATION REQUIRED:** Signed and acknowledged before a notary public with or without a jurat, depending on Form type; valid between parties and recordable.
- ✍ **PRIVATE SIGNATURE:** Signed by parties only; valid between parties, not recordable until acknowledged.
- 🚫 **ADMINISTRATIVE:** Internal or procedural form; no effect on ownership or title, and no notarization required.

FORM NO.	FORM TITLE	FORMALITY REQUIRED	AUTHORITY / NOTES
1.1–1.5	Foundational & Administrative Forms	✍ Private Signature (Notarization optional)	Corporate/administrative; NOT conveyances; cemetery authority internal acts.
2.1	Cemetery Space Purchase Agreement	✍ Private Signature (Acknowledgment optional)	**La. R.S. 8:909** (written contract required); not a conveyance of real rights.
2.2	Certificate of Transfer and Assignment of Interment Rights (Deed)	🖊 Notarization Required	Transfers interment rights but not immovable ownership; cemetery records require an acknowledged act.
2.3	Declaration of Assignment of Burial Spaces	🖊 Notarization Required (if by heir/seller)	Ensures evidentiary certainty; recommended for title chain.
2.4	Declaration of Inalienability of Cemetery Spaces	🖋 Authentic Act	Creates restriction/servitude. **C.C. arts. 708, 1833; R.S. 8:805.**
2.5	Testamentary Burial Space Designation	🖋 Authentic Act (Same form as Last Will and Testament)	Incorporated into a will/trust; not a stand-alone conveyance.
2.6	Codicil to Last Will and Testament	🖋 Authentic Act (Same form as Last Will and Testament)	As a codicil, serves as an addendum to a Last Will and Testament while ratifying all the provisions of the previous Last Will and Testament.
2.7	Cemetery Space Consignment Agreement	✍ Private Signature	Contractual agreement; no transfer of real rights.
2.8	Transfer & Assignment of Rights to Cemetery Authority for Credit	✍ Private Signature	Agreement between cemetery and owner; not required to be notarized.
2.9	Quitclaim Deed to Cemetery Rights	🖋 Authentic Act	**C.C. arts. 1833, 1836, 2440**; title-affecting instrument.
2.10	Act of Partition of Interment Rights	🖋 Authentic Act	Division of co-owned immovable real right. **C.C. art. 807, 1833.**

FORM NO.	FORM TITLE	FORMALITY REQUIRED	AUTHORITY / NOTES
2.11	Act of Exchange of Interment Rights	✍️ Private Signature	**C.C. art. 2660.** Exchange of real rights.
2.12	Dation en Paiement of Cemetery Space	🖋️ Authentic Act	**C.C. art. 2655**; conveyance in satisfaction of debt.
2.13	Promissory Note for Cemetery Interment Rights	✍️ Private Signature	Negotiable instrument; not a transfer of ownership.
2.14	Transfer & Assignment of Rights (Exchange Agreement)	✍️ Private Signature	Between the cemetery & the owner, does NOT require notarization.
2.15	Purchaser's Right of Cancellation Notice	✍️ Private Signature	Administrative notice; NOT required by statute; cemetery policy.
2.16	Purchaser's Notice – No Cancellation Period Exists	✍️ Private Signature	Clarifies policy; not required to be notarized.
2.17	Interment Order	✍️ Private Signature	Administrative authorization; no notarization.
2.18	Declaration of Interment Location for Owner	✍️ Private Signature	Owner direction; not a conveyance.
2.19	Cemetery Interment Record	🚫 No Notarization Required	Record-keeping document.
2.20	Affidavit of Lost or Destroyed Deed/Certificate	🖊️ Notarization Required	Affidavit – jurat required.
2.21	Assignment of Interment Rights (Sale)	🖊️ Notarization Required	Evidences transfer of burial rights.
2.22	Notice of Transfer or Sale to Cemetery Authority	✍️ Private Signature	Internal administrative filing.
2.23	Affidavit of Lost Proof of Purchase	🖊️ Notarization Required	Affidavit – must be sworn.
2.24	Cancellation & Refund Request Form	✍️ Private Signature	Administrative request to cemetery.
2.25	Act of Donation of Cemetery Space	🖋️ Authentic Act	**La. C.C. art. 1536; La. R.S. 8:803.**
2.26	Affidavit of Heirship (Disinterested Party)	🖊️ Notarization Required	Affidavit – evidentiary.
2.27	Waiver of Interment Rights (Family Member)	🖋️ Authentic Act	Relinquishes real right; **La. R.S. 8:812(B).**
3.1	Authorization for Interment	✍️ Private Signature	Administrative.

FORM NO.	FORM TITLE	FORMALITY REQUIRED	AUTHORITY / NOTES
3.2	Agreement for Temporary Interment	✍️ Private Signature	Administrative.
3.3	Authorization to Disinter or Reinter Human Remains	🖊️ Notarization Required	Public-health/chain-of-custody affidavit.
3.4	Certificate of Interment Completion	🚫 No Notarization Required	Cemetery-issued certificate.
3.5	Certification of Disinterment and Reinterment by Sexton	🚫 No Notarization Required	Cemetery-issued certificate.
3.6	Application for Disinterment / Reinterment	✍️ Private Signature	Administrative approval request.
3.7	Chain of Custody Record	✍️ Private Signature	Internal administrative log.
3.8	Notice of Proposed Disinterment	✍️ Private Signature	Notice; not a legal conveyance.
3.9	Certificate of Reinterment	🚫 No Notarization Required	Cemetery-issued certificate.
3.10	Cremated Remains Release Form	✍️ Private Signature	Administrative authorization.
3.11	Cemetery Work Permit / Contractor Work Order	✍️ Private Signature	Administrative.
4.1	Perpetual Care Agreement	✍️ Private Signature	Contract; no statutory notarial requirement.
4.2	Monthly Perpetual Care Fund Worksheet	🚫 No Notarization Required	Internal trust accounting.
4.3	Investment / Distribution Authorization	✍️ Private Signature	Trustee/cemetery administrative authorization.
4.4	Trustee Acknowledgment of Deposit	🚫 No Notarization Required	Acknowledgment receipt.
5.1	Notice of Abandoned Cemetery Space	✍️ Private Signature	Administrative notice.
5.2	Notice of Abandonment (Publication)	✍️ Private Signature	Administrative notice.
5.3	Certificate / Affidavit of Posting & Publication	🖊️ Notarization Required	Affidavit required under **La. R.S. 8:308 – 312.**

FORM NO.	FORM TITLE	FORMALITY REQUIRED	AUTHORITY / NOTES
5.4	Affidavit of No Response After Notice	🖊 Notarization Required	Evidentiary affidavit.
5.5	Board Resolution Declaring Space Abandoned	✍ Private Signature	Internal corporate act.
5.6	Application for Removal of Dedication	✍ Private Signature	Petition to court; no notarization.
5.7	Affidavit of Removal of Dedication	🖊 Notarization Required	Affidavit required by **La. R.S. 8:312.**
6.1	Sworn Statement of Facts	🖊 Notarization Required	Affidavit – must be sworn.
6.2	Witness Statement Form	🖊 Notarization Required	Sworn witness statement.
6.3	Declaration of Disposition of Remains	✍ Private Signature (Acknowledgment optional)	Not a conveyance; authorization only.
6.4	Declaration of Disposition of Remains Under a Mandate	🖊 Notarization Required	Because it is executed "under a mandate", jurat confirms principal's identity.

PART I

FOUNDATIONAL AND ADMINISTRATIVE FORMS

FORM 1.1

BOARD RESOLUTION AUTHORIZING EXECUTION OF CEMETERY DOCUMENTS

FORM: 🚫 **NO NOTARIZATION REQUIRED**

FORM REQUIREMENTS: This form generally does **not require notarization** unless the resolution itself will be recorded in parish conveyance records. It may be adopted and signed by board officers under the authority of the corporation. If recordation is intended, an **acknowledged signature before a notary** is recommended. It is **not an authentic act**, as it memorializes internal authorization rather than a conveyance.

PURPOSE: Confirms authorization from the governing board for designated officers to execute official documents on behalf of the Cemetery Authority.

CITATION: La. R.S. 8:305 – Dedication of Cemetery Property
"Every Cemetery Authority shall cause its dedication of property to be recorded in the conveyance records of the parish where the cemetery is situated."

DESCRIPTION: Used by the Cemetery Authority's board to formally grant legal signing authority to an executive officer or director. The resolution becomes part of the cemetery's permanent records for audit and title purposes.

RESOLUTION OF THE BOARD OF DIRECTORS / TRUSTEES

At a duly called meeting of the Board of Directors (or Trustees) of_____________________

Cemetery held on the _____ day of __________________, 20_____, at

____________________________, the following resolution was adopted:

BE IT RESOLVED, that ____ (Name and Title) is hereby authorized and empowered to execute on behalf of this Cemetery Authority all contracts, interment right certificates, perpetual care agreements, trust documents, or other official instruments required by law or policy, and to affix the seal of this authority thereto.

BE IT FURTHER RESOLVED, that this authorization shall remain in effect until revoked or superseded by a written resolution of this Board.

Adopted this _____ day of _____________, 20_______.

____

Signature of Chairperson

____

Printed Name of Chairperson

CERTIFICATION

I, the undersigned Secretary, do hereby certify that the foregoing resolution is a true and correct copy adopted by the governing body of the above-named Cemetery Authority at a duly convened meeting at which a quorum was present.

____

Signature of Secretary

____

Printed Name of Secretary

____

Date

FORM 1.2

CEMETERY RULES AND REGULATIONS ACKNOWLEDGMENT

FORM: 🚫 **NO NOTARIZATION REQUIRED**

FORM REQUIREMENTS: The form acknowledges receipt and acceptance of the cemetery's operating rules. It is executed under **private signature** for recordkeeping. If the acknowledgment will be attached to a recorded sale, it may be optionally **acknowledged before a notary** for evidentiary strength.

PURPOSE: Confirms that purchasers, families, or contractors have received and agree to comply with the cemetery's rules and regulations.

CITATION: La. R.S. 8:308 – Rules and Regulations of Cemetery Authorities
"Each Cemetery Authority may make, adopt, amend, add to, revise, or abolish rules and regulations for the use, care, control, management, restriction, and protection of all or any part of its cemetery and for the other purposes specified in this Title."

DESCRIPTION: Signed by the purchaser or family member at the time of purchase or burial to acknowledge awareness of the cemetery's operating policies. Serves as protection against disputes regarding maintenance, decoration, or conduct.

ACKNOWLEDGMENT OF CEMETERY RULES AND REGULATIONS

I, ____, the undersigned holder of rights of interment in the space(s) designated in the books of ____________ Cemetery as:

Building/Location	**Section**	**Row/Unit**	**Space No(s).**

acknowledge that I have received a copy of the Rules and Regulations of ________________________ Cemetery, that I have read and understand them, or have waived my right to read them, and that I agree to be bound by and comply with said Rules and Regulations, as they may be supplemented and amended from time to time.

Signed and agreed to this _______day of __________________, 20_____.

____
Signature of Interment Rights Holder

____
Printed Name

FORM 1.3

CERTIFICATION OF DEDICATION OR CONSECRATION OF CEMETERY GROUNDS (AFFIDAVIT)

FORM: ✐ **NOTARIZATION REQUIRED**

FORM REQUIREMENTS: A Certification of Dedication or Consecration of Cemetery Grounds does not require execution in authentic form, as it is a declaratory and evidentiary act rather than a conveyance of ownership or other immovable rights, under **La. R.S. 8:304 – 305**, the dedication of property for cemetery purposes occurs either through actual use for interments or by a written declaration filed in the parish conveyance records. This form serves to certify that the land has been dedicated or consecrated for cemetery use and is intended to provide public notice of this fact. A single signature by the cemetery authority, acknowledged before a notary public, is sufficient for recordation and evidentiary purposes. Authentic form may be used, but it is not required, since the document does not alter the title or create a new real right — it simply confirms that the property is subject to the statutory servitude of use as a cemetery.

PURPOSE: Declares that property has been formally dedicated for cemetery use and recorded in parish conveyance records.

CITATION: **La. R.S. 8:304 — Dedication of Property to Cemetery Purposes**
"Property dedicated to cemetery purposes shall be held and used exclusively for a cemetery and shall be recorded in the conveyance records of the parish in which the cemetery is located."

DESCRIPTION: Executed by the Cemetery Authority or property owner and filed in the parish conveyance office. This document provides permanent public evidence that the land is restricted to cemetery use in compliance with Louisiana law.

AFFIDAVIT OF DEDICATION OF CEMETERY GROUNDS

STATE OF LOUISIANA
PARISH OF ___________________________

BEFORE ME, the undersigned Notary Public, duly commissioned and qualified in and for the Parish and State aforesaid, PERSONALLY CAME AND APPEARED:

Affiant Name: ____

Title/Capacity: ____

Representing: ____

herein "Cemetery Authority,"

who, after being duly sworn, did depose and say:

That AFFIANT is duly authorized to act for and on behalf of the CEMETERY AUTHORITY named above and makes this affidavit in compliance with **La. R.S. 8:304-305**, for the purpose of **certifying the dedication of certain property for cemetery purposes**.

That the following described immovable property situated in the Parish of _____________________, State of Louisiana, has been acquired and set apart by the CEMETERY AUTHORITY for cemetery purposes:

Legal Description:

____

____

____

____

(Attach full legal DESCRIPTION of property or reference to recorded plat or survey.)

That said property has been and is hereby **dedicated exclusively to interment purposes** and shall be held, used, and maintained as cemetery grounds under the provisions of **Title 8 of the Louisiana Revised Statutes**, and that such dedication is made with the intent that the property shall be subject to all rights, duties, and protections provided therein.

That the CEMETERY AUTHORITY has full legal title and control of said property, and that the same shall be operated in accordance with all provisions of Louisiana cemetery law and regulations of the **Louisiana Cemetery Board**, including all requirements concerning perpetual care, recordkeeping, and trust fund compliance.

That once dedicated, said property shall not be used for any purpose other than as a cemetery, except as may be permitted under **La. R.S. 8:903 – 906** regarding removal of dedication, and only after lawful notice and approval by the proper authorities.

AFFIANT declares that this certification shall be recorded in the conveyance records of the Parish of ____________________________, and such recordation shall constitute public notice of the property's dedication as cemetery grounds.

AFFIANT acknowledges that all statements herein are true and correct to the best of AFFIANT'S knowledge, information, and belief, and AFFIANT understands that this affidavit is made under oath for the permanent record of the CEMETERY AUTHORITY and the Louisiana Cemetery Board.

AFFIANT:

____
Signature of Affiant

____
Printed Name of Affiant

____
Title/Capacity

____
For: (Cemetery Authority)

____
Date

SWORN TO AND SUBSCRIBED before me on this ____ day of ______________, 20____

____
Signature of Notary

Printed Notary Name: ______________________________
Notary ID or Bar Roll No.: ______________
My Commission is for Life

FORM 1.4

CEMETERY INTERMENT RIGHTS POLICY STATEMENT

FORM: 🚫 **NO NOTARIZATION REQUIRED**

FORM REQUIREMENTS: This is an internal policy instrument and does **not require notarization**. The Cemetery Authority may issue it as a certified copy or an administrative policy statement. If the cemetery wishes to establish it as an officially recorded regulation, an **acknowledged signature of the authority** is sufficient.

PURPOSE: Establishes written policies governing the issuance, ownership, transfer, and use of interment rights within the cemetery.

CITATION: La. R.S. 8:801 – Nature of Interment Right
"The right of interment is the right to use a cemetery space for the disposition of human remains and does not constitute ownership of real estate."

DESCRIPTION: Used to clarify to purchasers and heirs that the interment right is a limited privilege rather than a property interest. This document protects both the cemetery and the consumer by outlining rights and responsibilities under Title 8.

CEMETERY INTERMENT RIGHTS POLICY

This policy establishes the legal and administrative framework by which ______________________________ Cemetery grants and manages interment rights.

1. **Nature of Rights:**
   Interment rights confer only the privilege of burial or entombment in a designated space. Such rights do not constitute ownership of land or real property but are a servitude of use right under Louisiana law (**La. R.S. 8:801**).

2. **Transfer and Assignment:**
   Interment rights may be transferred or assigned only in accordance with cemetery regulations and upon proper written documentation approved by the Cemetery Authority.

3. **Abandonment and Reversion:**
   Failure to maintain contact or respond to notices for twenty-five (25) years may result in abandonment proceedings under **La. R.S. 8:903 – 905**, after which rights revert to the Cemetery Authority.

4. **Successor Rights:**
   Upon the death of the rights holder, interment rights pass to heirs-at-law or designated beneficiaries as provided by **La. R.S. 8:806 – 808**.

5. **Compliance:**
   All interment rights are subject to the Rules and Regulations of this cemetery and to all applicable provisions of Title 8 of the Louisiana Revised Statutes.

Executed and adopted this _____ day of ______________________, 20____, by order of the governing body of the CEMETERY AUTHORITY.

____

Signature of Authorized Representative

____

Title

FORM 1.5

ACT OF CORRECTION BY CEMETERY AUTHORITY

FORM: 🚫 **NO NOTARIZATION REQUIRED**

FORM REQUIREMENTS: This form does **not require notarization** because it is executed by the Cemetery Authority, not by a notary, and corrects administrative or typographical errors in cemetery records or previously issued certificates. If the correction is to be filed in the parish conveyance records, an **acknowledged signature by the cemetery's authorized representative** is recommended for authenticity. Still, the act does **not need to be in authentic form.** When used internally, it may remain a simple **act under private signature** maintained in the cemetery's permanent files.

PURPOSE: Corrects clerical or typographical errors in previously executed or recorded cemetery documents.

CITATION: La. R.S. 8:813 – Correction of Errors
"A Cemetery Authority shall have the right to correct any and all errors that may occur in or in connection with the operation of the cemetery, including without limitation those involving or in connection with the making of an interment, disinterment, or removal, or the DESCRIPTION, transfer, granting the right of use, or conveyance of a cemetery space, and in this connection, the Cemetery Authority shall have the right to substitute, grant the right of use, or convey, to correct any such errors, other interment rights, approximately equal in value and location as far as feasible, as selected by the authority; or, in the sole discretion of the authority, the correction of an error may be accomplished by the refunding of the amount of money paid on account of the acquisition or use of a cemetery space."

DESCRIPTION: Used when minor mistakes occur in recorded instruments such as names, lot numbers, or dates. Executed by the Cemetery Authority and filed to maintain accurate conveyance and ownership records.

ACT OF CORRECTION BY CEMETERY AUTHORITY

ON THE ____ day of ____________________, 20_____, __________________________ herein "Appearer," purchased from _____________________ Cemetery, herein "Cemetery Authority," a Right of Interment erroneously described as:

Building/Location	**Section**	**Row/Unit**	**Space No(s).**

On this day, the _____ day of ______________. 20____, the APPEARER does come before the CEMETERY AUTHORITY and authorizes an Act of Correction to amend the Contract and Deed to correct the DESCRIPTION of the purchased Cemetery burial rights location as:

Building/Location	**Section**	**Row/Unit**	**Space No(s).**

This correction is made in accordance with and fulfillment of **La. R.S 8:813**.

There are no payments or credits due in exchange for this correction.

__________________________________, APPEARER

Signature of Appearer

____

Printed Name of Appearer

____

Signature of Authorized Representative

____________________ CEMETERY, INC.

By __________________________________

Printed Name of Authorized Representative

ACT OF CORRECTION BY CEMETERY AUTHORITY

ON THE ____ day of ____________________, 20_____, __________________________ herein "Appearer," purchased from ______________________ Cemetery, herein "Cemetery Authority," a Right of interment in the space(s) designated in the books of ____________________Cemetery as:

Building/Location	**Section**	**Row/Unit**	**Space No(s).**

On this day, the _____ day of _______________. 20_____, the APPEARER does come before the CEMETERY AUTHORITY and authorizes an Act of Correction to amend the Contract and Deed to correct the following error(s):

____

____

____

____

All parties agree that error(s) shall be corrected as follows:

____

____

____

____

This correction is made in accordance with and fulfillment of **La. R.S 8:813**.
There are no payments or credits due in exchange for this correction.

____________________________________, APPEARER
Signature of Appearer

____
Printed Name of Appearer

____
Signature of Authorized Representative
FOR ______________________ CEMETERY, INC.
By ____________________________________
Printed Name of Authorized Representative

PART II

INTERMENT RIGHTS AND SALES

FORM 2.1

CEMETERY SPACE PURCHASE AGREEMENT (LAC §909 COMPLIANT)

FORM: 🚫 **NO NOTARIZATION REQUIRED**

FORM REQUIREMENTS: This form does **not require notarization** under **La. R.S. 8:812** or the Louisiana Administrative Code. It is a **private contract** between the purchaser and the Cemetery Authority and becomes enforceable upon signature alone. Although executed under private signature, this document is an **Authentic Act** under **La. R.S. 8:812.**

PURPOSE: Provides the written contract between the purchaser and Cemetery Authority for the sale of interment rights in compliance with Louisiana Administrative Code §909.

CITATION: La. Admin. Code tit. 46, Pt. XIII, §909 – Cemetery Sales Contracts; Required Contents
The following sample sales contract has the minimum required language as codified in **La. Admin. Code tit. 46, XIII-909**, namely:

1. Sequentially numbered
2. Date of the contract;
3. Name of the seller and purchaser;
4. Statement that the Cemetery is perpetual care, if applicable;
5. The location of the interment space;
6. An itemization of the prices charged, including any applied discounts, for each item provided as part of the contract;
7. The terms under which each contract is to be paid; and
8. The clear terms for cancellation of the agreement, including any damages for cancellation.
9. The cost of the cemetery space or interment right(s);
10. The type of interment to be provided and the number of interments allowed.
11. The amount or percentage to be placed in the Cemetery's perpetual or endowed care trust; and

12. A statement regarding whether the payment for the cemetery space(s) or interment right(s) includes or does not include the cost of opening and closing of the cemetery space.
13. The price of each item of merchandise or service contracted for.
14. If the merchandise will not be delivered or stored pursuant to **La. R.S. 8:502.1**; then, the agreement shall state the amount or percentage to be placed in the cemetery's merchandise trust fund.
15. A DESCRIPTION of each item of merchandise or service with sufficient information to describe the merchandise or service, including the size, design, and materials used in construction or manufacturing.

The sample form is intended solely to meet the minimum statutory requirements. Consult an attorney for further guidance if additional provisions are necessary for your Cemetery Authority.

DESCRIPTION: Used to document the sale of cemetery spaces. Ensures that all required disclosures—location, pricing, care trust details, and cancellation rights—are met to comply with state law and Louisiana Cemetery Board regulations.

CEMETERY PURCHASE AGREEMENT

Contract No.: ______________________________ Date: _________________________

This Cemetery Purchase Agreement, herein "Agreement," is made and entered into on the date shown above by and between:

SELLER / CEMETERY AUTHORITY:	**PURCHASER:**
Name: ________________	Name: ________________
Address: ________________	Address: ________________
City/State: ________________	City/State: ________________
Phone: ________________	Phone: ________________
Email: ________________	Email: ________________

LOCATION AND DESCRIPTION OF INTERMENT SPACE

Building/Location	**Section**	**Row/Unit**	**Space No(s).**

Type of Interment: ☐ In-ground ☐ Mausoleum ☐ Columbarium ☐ Other: ________________

PURCHASER acknowledges this is a right of interment only, not ownership of land, per **La. R.S. 8:801**.

ITEMIZATION OF PRICES (ALL CHARGES AND DISCOUNTS)

DESCRIPTION	Quantity	Unit Price	Discount	Total
Cemetery Space/Interment Rights		$		$
Opening and Closing Fees		$		$
Memorial, Marker, Monument		$		$
Other Burial Container / Vault		$		$
Other Merchandise (see below)		$		$
Other Fees / Services		$		$
		$		$
TOTAL CONTRACT PRICE				$

DESCRIPTION OF MERCHANDISE AND SERVICES

____

____

____

____

____

____

____

____

____

PERPETUAL CARE AND MERCHANDISE TRUST DEPOSITS

Perpetual Care Trust Fund:
☐ This cemetery is perpetual care. CEMETERY AUTHORITY shall deposit ___ % (minimum 10%) of the gross sales price into its perpetual care trust fund within 30 days after the close of the month of receipt, as required by **La. R.S. 8:454 and LAC 446: XIII 909**.

Merchandise Trust Fund:
☐ Not applicable (merchandise delivered at time of sale).
☐ Applicable — SELLER shall deposit ____ % (minimum 70%) of proceeds from undelivered merchandise into its merchandise trust fund pursuant to **La. R.S. 8:502.1** and **LAC 46: XIII 909(A)(14)**.

INCLUSION OF OPENING AND CLOSING FEES

☐ The purchase price includes the cost of opening and closing the interment space.
☐ The purchase price does not include the cost of opening and closing, which shall be billed separately at the rate in effect at the time of need.

TERMS OF PAYMENT

Payment Method: ☐ Paid in full ☐ Installments (attach schedule)
Deposit: $________ Balance: $________ Payments due monthly beginning ________ .Failure to pay within _____ days shall place purchaser in default as indicated below.

RIGHT OF CANCELLATION, DEFAULT, AND DAMAGES

☐ **Option A — Purchaser's Right to Cancel:**
PURCHASER may cancel this AGREEMENT within three (3) business days after execution by giving written notice to the CEMETERY AUTHORITY. Upon timely cancellation, all payments made shall be refunded in full, less any authorized administrative or trust fund costs.
If PURCHASER cancels this AGREEMENT after the three-day rescission period, the CEMETERY AUTHORITY may retain actual costs incurred plus up to ten percent (10%) of the purchase price as liquidated damages, provided such amount complies with Louisiana State Regulations. The CEMETERY AUTHORITY shall make all required adjustments to its trust fund deposits in accordance with **LAC 46: XIII.909(C)**.

☐ **Option B — No Right to Cancel:**
PURCHASER acknowledges and agrees that this AGREEMENT is final upon execution and that no right of cancellation or rescission is granted. All payments made are subject to the terms of this AGREEMENT and applicable Louisiana law, and the CEMETERY AUTHORITY shall make all required adjustments to its trust fund deposits in accordance with **LAC 46: XIII.909(C)**.

GOVERNING LAW

This AGREEMENT shall be governed by the laws of the State of Louisiana, including **La. R.S. Title 8** and **La. Admin. Code tit. 46, Pt. XIII**.

ACKNOWLEDGMENTS

PURCHASER acknowledges receipt of: written price list of all cemetery property and services, copy of this fully executed AGREEMENT, copy of the Cemetery's Rules and Regulations, and disclosure of trust fund requirements and right of cancellation as outlined above.

SIGNATURES

Purchaser: ____ Date: ______________

Co-Purchaser (if any): _________________________________ Date: ______________

Authorized Cemetery Representative: _____________________ Date: ______________

FORM 2.2

CERTIFICATE OF TRANSFER AND ASSIGNMENT OF INTERMENT RIGHTS (DEED)

FORM: 🚫 **NO NOTARIZATION REQUIRED**

FORM REQUIREMENTS: Since this form conveys interment rights by the Cemetery Authority to an owner, it is not required to be notarized under Louisiana law.

PURPOSE: Records the lawful conveyance of interment rights from the Cemetery Authority to a purchaser or from one private owner to another.

CITATION: **La. R.S. 8:801 – Nature of Interment Right**
"The right of interment is the right to use a cemetery space for the disposition of human remains and does not constitute ownership of real estate."

DESCRIPTION: Acts as the official certificate or "deed" of ownership for interment rights. The Cemetery Authority signs and issues this document to purchasers or transferees to confirm legal entitlement to the space.

______________________________Cemetery No __________

____

____

CERTIFICATE OF TRANSFER AND ASSIGNMENT

KNOW ALL MEN BY THESE PRESENTS: that __________ Cemetery, Inc., a Louisiana corporation, herein "Grantor," for and in consideration of the sum of

____ ($__________________) Dollars,

Issued in the name of ___________________________________ herein "Grantee," does hereby grant, bargain, sell and convey to the GRANTEE, his/her heirs and assigns forever, a right of interment in the following space(s):

Building/Location	**Section**	**Row/Unit**	**Space No(s).**

Erected for the GRANTOR in ____________________ Cemetery, situated in the Parish of ____________________ and State of Louisiana, together with all appurtenances thereto belonging.

To have and to hold the use of the above granted space(s) to the GRANTEE, his/her heirs and assigns forever, subject however to the laws of the state, and to the conditions and restrictions contained in the rules and regulations of __________________Cemetery Inc., now in force or which may be herein adopted and the GRANTOR hereby covenants to and with the GRANTEE, his/her heirs and assigns, that it is lawfully seized of the above granted premises, and has good right to sell and convey the use of the same for the purpose above expressed.

GRANTOR warrants that ten percent (10%) of the above recited consideration has been set aside and placed in a trust, and the income from said trust fund shall be used for the general care and maintenance of said space(s). GRANTOR'S liability is limited to the income from said trust fund.

In Witness Whereof ________________ Cemetery, Inc. has caused this instrument to be signed by its designated representative and affixed the corporate seal of _______________ Cemetery, Inc. in the Parish of __________________, State of Louisiana, on the _____day of ____________ in the year of our Lord __________.

________________________ CEMETERY, INC.

By: ____________________________________

Signature of Authorized Representative

FORM 2.3

DECLARATION OF ASSIGNMENT OF BURIAL SPACES (NOTARIAL AND NON-NOTARIAL)

FORM: 🚫 **NO NOTARIZATION REQUIRED**

FORM REQUIREMENTS: The **notarial version** should be executed as an **acknowledged act** before a Louisiana notary to ensure evidentiary validity under **La. R.S. 8:803,** but this is not legally required. The **non-notarial version** may be signed under private signature and kept in the cemetery's files, but notarization is advisable if disputes or recordation are anticipated.

PURPOSE: Allows an owner of interment rights to designate who may be buried in specific spaces.

CITATION: **La. R.S. 8:803 – Use of Interment Space**
"The person having the right of interment in a cemetery space may determine who may be interred therein, and the Cemetery Authority shall permit interment in accordance with such written authorization."

DESCRIPTION: Enables an interment rights owner to assign designated spaces to family members. May be notarized or executed under penalty of perjury and filed with the cemetery to govern interment permissions.

NOTARIAL DECLARATION OF ASSIGNMENT OF BURIAL SPACES

STATE OF LOUISIANA
PARISH OF ____________________________

BE IT KNOWN, that on this _____day of ___________________, 20 _____ before me, the undersigned Notary Public, PERSONALLY CAME AND APPEARED:

___________________________________, of the age of majority and a resident of the Parish of ___________________, State of Louisiana, who declared:

That AFFIANT is the lawful owner of _______ (___) rights of interment in burial spaces located within ___________________ Cemetery, situated in the Parish of ___________________, State of Louisiana, more particularly described as follows:

Building/Location	**Section**	**Row/Unit**	**Space No(s).**

herein "Burial Space No. 1,"

Building/Location	**Section**	**Row/Unit**	**Space No(s).**

herein "Burial Space No. 2,"

Building/Location	**Section**	**Row/Unit**	**Space No(s).**

herein "Burial Space No. 3,"

Designation of Interments

AFFIANT hereby designates that the following persons are permitted to be interred in said burial spaces, one person per space, unless otherwise permitted by CEMETERY Rules and Regulations:

BURIAL SPACE NO. 1 shall be reserved for ________________________________.

BURIAL SPACE NO. 2 shall be reserved for ________________________________.

BURIAL SPACE NO. 3 shall be reserved for ________________________________.

Future Ownership and Disposition

In accordance with **La. R.S. 8:805**, AFFIANT declares his or her intention concerning the ownership and descent of the above-described burial spaces in the event that any of the designated individuals are not interred therein.

AFFIANT has this day selected and initiated **one** of the following declarations:

(Declarant shall initial one option only)

☐ ______ **Inalienable Declaration:** The designated burial spaces are hereby declared *inalienable* and may not be transferred or otherwise disposed of except as provided by law.

☐ ______ **Descend to Heirs Declaration:** If any of the designated individuals are not interred in their assigned spaces, such unused burial spaces shall *descend to my heirs or assigns* of the according to law.

Effect of Declaration

This declaration shall serve as an expression of the owner's intent under **La. R.S. 8:805** and shall be binding upon the DECLARANT, his or her heirs, successors, and assigns. A copy shall be filed with the records of ____________________ Cemetery.

DECLARANT:

____
Signature of Declarant

____
Printed Name of Declarant

SWORN TO AND SUBSCRIBED before me on
this ____ day of ______________, 20____

____
Signature of Notary

Printed Notary Name: ______________________________
Notary ID or Bar Roll No.: ______________
My Commission is for Life

DECLARATION OF ASSIGNMENT OF BURIAL SPACES

STATE OF LOUISIANA
PARISH OF ___________________________

I, ____, of the age of majority and a resident of the Parish of ____________________, State of Louisiana, being of sound mind and acting freely and voluntarily, do hereby make this declaration pursuant to **La. R.S. 8:805**, for the purpose of designating the persons entitled to interment in certain burial spaces where I own interment rights in ____________________ Cemetery, located in the Parish of ____________________, Louisiana.

Declaration of Ownership

I am the lawful owner of _______ (___) rights of interment in burial spaces located within ____________________ Cemetery, situated in the Parish of ____________________, State of Louisiana, more particularly described as follows:

Building/Location	**Section**	**Row/Unit**	**Space No(s).**

herein "Burial Space No. 1,"

Building/Location	**Section**	**Row/Unit**	**Space No(s).**

herein "Burial Space No. 2,"

Building/Location	**Section**	**Row/Unit**	**Space No(s).**

herein "Burial Space No. 3,"

Designation of Interments

I hereby designate that the following persons are permitted to be interred in said burial spaces, one person per space, unless otherwise permitted by CEMETERY Rules and Regulations:

BURIAL SPACE NO. 1 shall be reserved for ____.

BURIAL SPACE NO. 2 shall be reserved for ____.

BURIAL SPACE NO. 3 shall be reserved for ____.

Future Ownership and Disposition

Pursuant to **La. R.S. 8:805**, I declare my intention regarding the ownership of these burial spaces in the event that any of the above-designated individuals are not interred therein. I have selected and initialed **one** of the following options:

(Declarant shall initial one option only)

______ **Inalienable Declaration:** The designated burial spaces are hereby declared *inalienable* and may not be transferred or otherwise disposed of except as provided by law.

☐ ______ **Descend to Heirs Declaration:** If any of the designated individuals are not interred in their assigned spaces, such unused burial spaces shall *descend to my heirs or assigns* of the according to law.

Effect of Declaration

This declaration shall serve as an expression of the owner's intent under **La. R.S. 8:805** and shall be binding upon the Declarant, his or her heirs, successors, and assigns. A copy shall be filed with the records of ____________________ Cemetery.

Executed at __________________, Louisiana, on this ____ day of ________________, 20 _____.

DECLARANT:

____
Signature of Declarant

____
Printed Name of Declarant

FORM 2.4

DECLARATION OF INALIENABILITY OF CEMETERY SPACES

FORM: ✏️ **NOTARIZATION REQUIRED**

FORM REQUIREMENTS: This declaration **should be notarized** as an **acknowledged act**, because it restricts transfer that binds heirs and successors. It is filed in the cemetery's official records and often recorded. An authentic act is **not required**, but notarization is best practice for a binding effect.

PURPOSE: Declares that certain cemetery spaces are inalienable and may not be transferred outside the family.

CITATION: La. R.S. 8:805 – Transfer or Assignment of Interment Rights
"A family may agree that the cemetery spaces it owns shall be inalienable, and such declaration shall be binding upon all heirs and assigns when recorded in the cemetery's records."

DESCRIPTION: Used by families to preserve burial grounds for lineage or heritage reasons. Once executed and recorded with the cemetery, the inalienability binds future heirs.

DECLARATION OF INALIENABILITY OF CEMETERY SPACES

STATE OF LOUISIANA
PARISH OF IBERIA

BE IT KNOWN, that on this ___ day of _______________, 20_____,

BEFORE ME, the undersigned Notary Public, duly commissioned and qualified in and for the Parish and State aforesaid, PERSONALLY CAME AND APPEARED:

____________________________, a person of the age of majority and a domiciliary of _________________________ Parish, Louisiana, who did declare as follows:

That he is the owner of interment rights in the following cemetery spaces located in _____________________ Cemetery, situated in ____________________, Louisiana and that:

Building/Location	**Section**	**Row/Unit**	**Space No(s).**

is designated for the interment of _______________________________
(Relationship: ____)

Building/Location	**Section**	**Row/Unit**	**Space No(s).**

is designated for the interment of _______________________________
(Relationship: ____)

Building/Location	**Section**	**Row/Unit**	**Space No(s).**

is designated for the interment of _______________________________
(Relationship: ____)

It is his or her express will and intention that the above-named interment rights be and are hereby declared inalienable, meaning that they shall not be sold, transferred, donated, assigned, leased, mortgaged, or otherwise disposed of, and shall remain permanently reserved for the interment of the above-named individuals or their remains.

This declaration of inalienability is made pursuant to **La. R.S. 8:805**. Should any individual designated for a specific cemetery space be interred elsewhere, and no human remains are interred in the respective space, then that cemetery space shall pass according to the laws of intestate succession of the State of Louisiana. The heirs, as determined by law, shall have the right to sell or otherwise transfer said cemetery space, provided it remains unoccupied.

AFFIANT:

____

Signature of Affiant

______________________________, AFFIANT

Printed name of Affiant

SWORN TO AND SUBSCRIBED before me on this ____ day of _______________, 20____

____

Signature of Notary

Printed Notary Name: _______________________________

Notary ID or Bar Roll No.: _______________

My Commission is for Life

FORM 2.5

TESTAMENTARY BURIAL SPACE DESIGNATION (TRUST CLAUSE OR WILL PROVISION)

FORM: AUTHENTIC FORM REQUIRED (SPECIAL FORM)

FORM REQUIREMENTS: When included in a will or trust, it follows the formalities of that instrument. A will must be in **statutory or notarial form** under **La. C.C. art. 1577 et seq.**, and a trust clause must be **authentic** under **La. R.S. 9:1752**. If executed separately, notarization is recommended for evidentiary strength. If in the Last Will and Testament, ensure that the Testator signs every page.

PURPOSE: Provides a clause for inclusion in a will or trust to identify which heirs will hold burial privileges.

CITATION: **La. R.S. 8 § 803 – Descent of title to cemetery space.**
"Except as otherwise provided in this Chapter, every right of interment and cemetery space shall be subject to the laws of this state pertaining to community property, inheritance, including but not limited to the laws of intestacy, donations inter vivos and mortis causa, and successions."

DESCRIPTION: This model clause ensures that upon the death of the owner, the designated successors are lawfully recognized. It prevents disputes over family burial rights and provides clear instructions for succession.

TESTAMENTARY BURIAL SPACE DESIGNATION

(TRUST CLAUSE OR WILL PROVISION)

I direct and establish a *Testamentary Burial Space Designation Trust* as follows:

Purpose.

The sole and exclusive purpose of this trust is to designate, in accordance with **La. R.S. 8:805**, the persons who shall have the right of interment within the unoccupied portions of my interment rights in burial spaces located in ________________________________ Cemetery, Parish of ____________________, State of Louisiana.

Spaces Covered.

This trust applies to interment rights in the burial spaces owned by me and described as follows:

Building/Location	**Section**	**Row/Unit**	**Space No(s).**

1. **Certificate or Title No. (if applicable):** ______________________________

2. **Designated Persons for Interment.**

   The following persons shall have the right of interment in the unoccupied portions of my burial property, one person per space, unless otherwise permitted by cemetery regulations:

   1. ____
      (Relationship: ______________________________)
   2. ____
      (Relationship: ______________________________)
   3. ____
      (Relationship: ______________________________)
   4. ____
      (Relationship: ______________________________)

   If any of the persons named above should be interred elsewhere, decline interment, or predecease me, their respective right of interment shall lapse, and the space shall remain available to my lawful heirs, to be assigned by the Trustee in accordance with this instrument and **La. R.S. 8:805**.

Burial Space Inalienability

☐ ______ **Inalienable Declaration:** The designated burial spaces are hereby declared *inalienable* and may not be transferred or otherwise disposed of except as provided by law.

☐ ______ **Descend to Heirs Declaration:** If any of the designated individuals are not interred in their assigned spaces, such unused burial spaces shall *descend to my heirs or assigns* of the according to law.

Trustee.
I appoint the natural person then serving as Director, Sexton, or Manager of ________________________ Cemetery, located in the Parish of ________________________, State of Louisiana, to act as Trustee of this Burial Space Designation Trust, together with all successors in said office, who shall serve by virtue of their position.

Duties of Trustee.
The Trustee's sole duties are to:

- Hold legal title to my burial property in trust solely for the limited purpose of honoring this designation;
- Maintain a written record of the persons named herein;
- Communicate these designations to the Cemetery Authority and provide copies of this clause to the cemetery's records; and
- Execute, if requested, any declaration or affidavit required by the cemetery to confirm the designated interment rights.

The Trustee shall have no power to sell, mortgage, or otherwise transfer any right or interest in the burial spaces except as authorized by law.

Duration.
This trust shall continue until all designated spaces are occupied, or until the cemetery's dedication is removed or altered under **La. R.S. 8:903 et seq.**, whichever occurs first. Upon completion or termination, the trust shall automatically extinguish, and any residual rights shall revert to my lawful heirs.

Interpretation.
This trust shall be liberally construed to carry out my express intent that the persons named above shall have the right of interment in the burial property described herein. No other purpose, management, or financial obligation is created by this clause.

FORM 2.6

CODICIL TO LAST WILL AND TESTAMENT

FORM: ✒ **AUTHENTIC FORM REQUIRED (SPECIAL FORM)**

FORM REQUIREMENTS: A codicil follows the formalities of a Last Will and Testament. A will must be in **statutory or notarial form** under **La. C.C. art. 1577 et seq.**, and so this codicil follows that form. Ensure that the testator signs at the bottom of every page of this codicil.

PURPOSE: This codicil designates control of burial rights to another person as part of the Last Will and Testament

CITATION: **La. R.S. 8 § 803 – Descent of title to cemetery space.**
"Except as otherwise provided in this Chapter, every right of interment and cemetery space shall be subject to the laws of this state pertaining to community property, inheritance, including but not limited to the laws of intestacy, donations inter vivos and mortis causa, and successions."

DESCRIPTION: This codicil ensures that upon the owner's death, the designated persons have control of the burial space as the owner deemed. It prevents disputes over family burial rights and provides clear instructions for succession.

STATE OF LOUISIANA
PARISH OF ________________________

CODICIL TO LAST WILL AND TESTAMENT

OF

____

I, ________________________, **am of the full age of majority, able to comprehend generally the nature and consequences of my actions, and understand the disposition I am making, and am acting freely and voluntarily, without duress, fraud, or undue influence,** and do hereby make this codicil to my last will and testament which is dated ________________________, and is expressly not revoked but continues in force, subject to the addition(s) below. I confirm that no other codicils to my last will and testament have been made previously.

Notwithstanding any provision of this Codicil to the contrary, I expressly **reserve unto myself the exclusive, superior, and non-delegable right to be buried, entombed, or interred in the cemetery space described below**.

No person, including ________________________ or ________________________, shall have authority to prohibit, delay, redirect, or override my own right of interment in said cemetery space.

It is my express intent that this reservation **shall take precedence over all other grants of authority** contained in this Codicil.

Subject always to the reservation set forth above, I hereby give, devise, and bequeath to

________________________, whose mailing address is ______________________________,

all of my right, title, and interest in and to the exclusive authority to control burial, interment, entombment, cremation placement, memorialization, and all other rights of interment, within the meaning of Louisiana Civil Code articles 870 through 874, with respect to the following cemetery space located at _______________**Cemetery**, located in ______________, Louisiana:

Building/Location	**Section**	**Row/Unit**	**Space No(s).**

This grant includes, without limitation, the exclusive right to:

____
Testator Signature

1. Determine **who may be buried, entombed, or interred** in said cemetery space *(other than myself)*;
2. Determine the **order and manner of interments** *(subject to my reserved right of first interment)*;
3. Consent to or prohibit any **disinterment, reinterment, relocation, or transfer**;
4. Approve or reject any **memorials, inscriptions, markers, or monuments** associated with said cemetery space;
5. Execute any documents or authorizations required by _______________ **Cemetery** or any governmental authority; and
6. Exercise all other rights of interment recognized under Louisiana law.

It is my express intent that ___________________ **shall be the sole and exclusive person vested with authority over all burial and interment decisions** concerning the above-described cemetery space, subject always to my reserved right of interment.

In the event that ____:

- predeceases me,
- declines to act,
- is unwilling or unable to act,
- cannot be located within a reasonable time after my death, or
- is legally incapacitated,

then I hereby give, devise, and bequeath **all of the same burial, interment, and rights of interment authority described above** to:

________________________, whose mailing address is ________________________________,

who shall thereupon have the same sole and exclusive authority to control burial, interment, entombment, cremation placement, memorialization, and all other rights of interment with respect to the above-described cemetery space, to the same extent and with the same force and effect as if originally granted to her herein, **subject always to my reserved right of interment set forth above.**

It is my express intent that:

- ______________________________, as primary authority, and
- ______________________________, as successor authority,

____
Testator Signature

shall be the **only persons vested with authority** over all burial and interment decisions concerning the above-described cemetery space, **other than my own reserved right of interment**.

No other heir, legatee, forced heir, beneficiary, executor, administrator, or family member shall have any right to control, interfere with, contest, or override the decisions of the person then holding authority under this Codicil.

Any provision of my Original Will or any prior codicil that purports to grant burial rights, interment authority, or rights of interment in the above-described cemetery space to any person other than ______________________________ or ______________________________, as provided herein, is hereby revoked and replaced by this Codicil.

This Codicil is intended to transfer **authority and rights of interment only** and is not intended to:

1. Transfer ownership of any human remains; or
2. Create any ownership interest in immovable property beyond such burial and interment rights as are recognized under Louisiana law and the rules and regulations of ___________________________Cemetery.

I expressly authorize __________________ **Cemetery**, ____________________, Louisiana, and its officers, employees, and agents to:

1. Rely conclusively upon this Codicil as establishing burial and interment authority and my reserved right of interment;
2. Rely upon the written declaration or affidavit of ___________________ or ___________________, or upon a death certificate or written certification of incapacity or unavailability of ____________________, in determining successor burial authority in favor of ____________________; and
3. Act without further duty to investigate or adjudicate competing family claims.

___________________ Cemetery shall incur **no liability** for honoring the instructions or decisions of the person then holding authority under this Codicil or for honoring my reserved right of interment, in good faith.

Except as expressly modified by this Codicil, I hereby ratify, confirm, and republish my Original Will in all respects

____
(Signature of Testator)

_________________________, Testator
(Printed Name of Testator)

____
Testator Signature

In our presence the testator has declared or signified that this instrument is his or her codicil, that it is the intention to make this amendment to his or her last will and testament, that the codicil does make those changes, additions or deletions which he or she desires to make, and that the testator has signed it at the end and on each other separate page, and in the presence of the testator and each other we have hereunto subscribed our names this _____ day of _____________________, 20____.

WITNESSES:

____

Print Name: ______________________________

____

Print Name: ______________________________

____

Signature of Notary

Printed Notary Name: _________________________

Notary ID or Bar Roll No.: _______________

My Commission is for Life

____

Testator Signature

FORM 2.7

CEMETERY SPACE CONSIGNMENT AGREEMENT

FORM: 🚫 **NO NOTARIZATION REQUIRED**

FORM REQUIREMENTS: A private contractual form that does **not require notarization.** It may be signed under private signature between the owner and the Cemetery Authority. If the owner wishes to record the transaction for evidentiary or resale purposes, a **notarial acknowledgment** is optional but not mandated.

PURPOSE: Allows a space owner to return unused rights to the Cemetery Authority for resale under agreed terms.

CITATION: La. R.S. 8:306 – Resale and Reacquisition of Interment Spaces
"A Cemetery Authority may sell or resell interment spaces and may enter into contracts concerning their resale under terms consistent with its rules."

DESCRIPTION: Used when interment rights owner wishes to consign an unused space for resale by the cemetery. The agreement specifies resale price, commission, and refund distribution upon sale.

CEMETERY SPACE CONSIGNMENT AGREEMENT

This Agreement is made on this _____ day of ______________, 20______, by and between:

Name: ____
Address: ____,
herein "Consignor," and

_________________________________ **Cemetery**
Address: ____,
herein "Consignee;"

CONSIGNOR is the lawful holder of interment rights in the space(s) designated in the books of ___________________ Cemetery as:

Building/Location	**Section**	**Row/Unit**	**Space No(s).**

herein "Consigned Space," in the aforesaid Cemetery. CONSIGNOR authorizes the CONSIGNER to offer the CONSIGNED SPACE for resale under the Cemetery's standard pricing policy. Upon sale, the Cemetery Authority shall remit to CONSIGNOR the sum of _________________________________ ($________________) or _____% of the sales price. (agreed resale price or percentage).

This consignment shall remain in effect for ______ **months** from the date of execution unless revoked in writing with thirty (30) days' notice by either party. CONSIGNEE shall have the exclusive right of consignment during this term.

All resale transactions shall comply with **La. R.S. 8:802** and shall be documented by a new purchase agreement and certificate of interment rights.

Upon notice to the CONSIGNOR by CONSIGNEE that burial rights have been sold, this agreement shall serve as an automatic transfer of all rights, title, and interest in the CONSIGNED SPACE(s) from CONSIGNOR to CONSIGNEE.

CONSIGNOR:

____
Signature of Consignor

____
Printed Name of Consignor

CONSIGNEE (Cemetery Authority)

____
Signature of Consignee

____
Printed Name of Consignee

FORM 2.8

TRANSFER AND ASSIGNMENT OF INTERMENT RIGHTS TO CEMETERY AUTHORITY FOR CREDIT

FORM: 🚫 **NO NOTARIZATION REQUIRED**

FORM REQUIREMENTS: This is a transaction between the space owner and the Cemetery Authority. The signed agreement alone is sufficient for re-issuance or credit.

PURPOSE: Permits an owner to return previously purchased spaces to the cemetery in exchange for credit or refund.

CITATION: **La. R.S. 8:306(B) – Resale and Reacquisition of Interment Spaces**
"A Cemetery Authority may repurchase or accept assignment of interment rights and may issue credit or refund to the owner under conditions set forth in the contract or rules."

DESCRIPTION: Used when an owner no longer wishes to retain interment rights and desires credit toward another purchase. Both parties sign and retain copies for permanent record.

TRANSFER AND ASSIGNMENT OF INTERMENT RIGHTS TO CEMETERY AUTHORITY FOR CREDIT

This Transfer and Assignment of Cemetery Interment Rights, herein "Agreement," is made and entered into this _____ day of __________, 20 _______, by and between:

____

____

____ herein "Assignor," and

____

____

____ herein "Cemetery Authority" or "Assignee,"

RECITALS

WHEREAS, the ASSIGNOR is the lawful owner of the rights of interment in _________________ Cemetery, in the Parish of ____________, Louisiana, designated in the books of _____________________ Cemetery as:

Building/Location	**Section**	**Row/Unit**	**Space No(s).**

WHEREAS the ASSIGNOR desires to transfer and assign all rights, title, and interest in the above-described cemetery space(s) to the ASSIGNEE.

NOW, THEREFORE, for and in consideration of the following terms and conditions, the ASSIGNOR hereby transfers, conveys, and assigns all right, title, and interest in and to the above-described cemetery space(s) to the ASSIGNEE, its successors, and assigns, to have and hold forever.

TERMS AND CONDITIONS

1. **Transfer of Title**: The ASSIGNOR warrants that the cemetery space(s) described above are free from any encumbrances and that the ASSIGNOR has the full right to transfer and assign the title to the ASSIGNEE.
2. **Assumption of Rights**: The ASSIGNEE assumes all rights, responsibilities, and obligations associated with the cemetery space(s) upon the execution of this Agreement.
3. **Payment**: The Assignee agrees to credit the ASSIGNOR the sum of ____ Dollars ($____________) as full consideration for this transfer and assignment.
4. **Effective Date**: This Transfer and Assignment of Interment Rights shall be effective immediately upon execution by both parties.
5. **Acknowledgment of Cemetery Management**: Both the ASSIGNOR and ASSIGNEE acknowledge that the cemetery management has been notified of this transfer and has given their consent, if required, for the transfer of the interment rights. The transfer may require the completion of additional paperwork with the cemetery administration.

EXECUTION

The ASSIGNOR and ASSIGNEE have executed this Transfer and Assignment of Interment Rights as of the day and year first above written.

ASSIGNOR	**ASSIGNEE**
______________________________	______________________________
Signature of Assignor	Signature of Authorized Cemetery Representative
______________________________	______________________________
Printed Name of Assignor	Printed Name of Authorized Cemetery Representative

FORM 2.9

QUITCLAIM DEED TO CEMETERY RIGHTS

FORM: **AUTHENTIC FORM REQUIRED**

FORM REQUIREMENTS: A quitclaim is a formal release and conveyance of any rights held by the grantor in a cemetery space, and Louisiana law requires such acts to be made before a **notary public and two witnesses** in accordance with **La. C.C. art. 1833 et seq.** The authentic form verifies the vendor and vendee's identity and intent, provides protection against later disputes, and ensures recordability in the cemetery's or parish's conveyance records.

PURPOSE: Transfers whatever interment rights the grantor may hold in a designated cemetery space to another person or to the Cemetery Authority, **without warranty** of title.

CITATION: **La. C.C. art. 2502 — Transfer of rights to a thing**
"A person may transfer to another whatever rights to a thing he may then have, without warranting the existence of any such rights. In such a case, the transferor does not owe restitution of the price to the transferee in the event of eviction, nor may that transfer be rescinded for lesion. Such a transfer does not give rise to a presumption of bad faith on the part of the transferee and is a just title for the purposes of acquisitive prescription."

DESCRIPTION: Use this deed when the current holder releases and conveys any and all interment rights they may have, **as-is and without warranty**, to the grantee or back to the cemetery. It's appropriate for corrective transfers, settlements, or where chain-of-title certainty cannot be assured. The cemetery records the quitclaim with its ownership register and may (optionally) reference it in parish conveyance records for completeness.

*** See Appendix for various forms of appearance clauses that can be used**

QUITCLAIM DEED TO CEMETERY RIGHTS

STATE OF LOUISIANA
PARISH OF ______________________

BE IT KNOWN, that on this _____ day of _____, 20_____, before me, the undersigned Notary Public, duly commissioned in and for the Parish and state aforesaid, and in the presence of the witnesses herein named and undersigned: PERSONALLY, CAME AND APPEARED:

____ a ☐ single ☐ married ☐ widowed ☐ divorced (circle one) person, of the full age of majority, domiciled in and a resident of the Parish of __________________________, State of Louisiana, whose permanent mailing address is ____, and who declares unto me that he/she ☐ has never been married / ☐ has been married but once, to ____________________________________, from whom he/she was divorced in __________________ Parish, on ______________________, herein "Vendor,"

AND

____ a ☐ single ☐ married ☐ widowed ☐ divorced (circle one) person, of the full age of majority, domiciled in and a resident of the Parish of __________________________, State of Louisiana, whose permanent mailing address is ____, and who declares unto me that he/she ☐ has never been married / ☐ has been married but once, to ____________________________________, from whom he/she was divorced in __________________ Parish, on ______________________, herein "Vendee,"

WHEREAS VENDOR is the listed co-owner in indivision of rights to interment in a certain space designated in the books of ___________________ Cemetery as:

Building/Location	**Section**	**Row/Unit**	**Space No(s).**

herein "Space A,"

WHEREAS VENDEE is the listed co-owner in indivision of rights to interment in a certain space designated in the books of ___________________ Cemetery as:

Building/Location	**Section**	**Row/Unit**	**Space No(s).**

herein "Space B,"

NOW, THEREFORE, for and in consideration of the mutual covenants and agreements herein contained, the parties do hereby agree as follows:

1. **Quitclaim by Vendor:** VENDOR does hereby remise, release, quitclaim, and forever convey unto VENDEE all right, title, and interest in and to SPACE A together with all privileges and appurtenances thereunto belonging or in anywise appertaining.
2. **Quitclaim by Vendee:** VENDEE does hereby remise, release, quitclaim, and forever convey unto VENDOR all right, title, and interest in and to SPACE B, together with all privileges and appurtenances thereunto belonging or in anywise appertaining.
3. **"As Is" Condition:** The exchange is made "AS IS" and without warranty of any kind, either express or implied, except as to authority and title.
4. **Binding Effect:** This agreement shall be binding upon and inure to the benefit of the parties hereto, their heirs, successors, and assigns.

THUS, DONE, SIGNED, AND PASSED on the day and date first above mentioned, in the presence of the undersigned competent witnesses, who hereunto sign their names with the said appearers and me, Notary, after due reading of the whole.

WITNESSES:

____
Signature of Witness

____
Printed Name of Witness

____
Signature of Witness

____
Printed Name of Witness

VENDOR:

____
Signature of Vendor

____
Printed Name of Vendor

VENDEE:

____
Signature of Vendee

____
Printed Name of Vendee

____
Signature of Notary

Printed Notary Name: ______________________

Notary ID or Bar Roll No.: __________

My Commission is for Life

FORM 2.10

ACT OF PARTITION OF INTERMENT RIGHTS

FORM: 🖋 **AUTHENTIC FORM REQUIRED**

FORM REQUIREMENTS: A partition divides interment rights among heirs or co-owners and has the effect of conveying each party's interest. Under **La. C.C. arts. 1833 and 1839**, such acts require execution before a **notary public and two witnesses**. The authentic form ensures that the parties' identities and consent are verified and that the instrument can be safely recorded in the cemetery's or parish's conveyance records.

PURPOSE: Divides jointly owned interment rights among co-owners or heirs.

CITATION: La. R.S. 8:805(B) – Partition of Interment Rights
"When two or more persons are joint owners of interment rights, they may agree in writing to partition the cemetery spaces among themselves, and the Cemetery Authority shall record such partition."

DESCRIPTION: Executed among heirs or multiple owners to clearly allocate specific spaces. This process prevents conflicts by identifying who controls each burial location.

*** See Appendix for various forms of appearance clauses that can be used.**

ACT OF PARTITION OF INTERMENT RIGHTS

STATE OF LOUISIANA
PARISH OF ____________________

BEFORE ME, the undersigned Notary Public, duly commissioned and qualified in and for the state and parish aforesaid, and in the presence of the two witnesses whose names are hereunto subscribed, PERSONALLY CAME and appeared:

____________________________________ a ☐ single ☐ married ☐ widowed ☐ divorced (circle one) person, of the full age of majority, domiciled in and a resident of the Parish of ________________________, State of Louisiana, whose permanent mailing address is ____, and who declares unto me that he/she ☐ has never been married / ☐ has been married but once, to ____________________________________, from whom he/she was divorced in _________________ Parish, on _____________________, herein "Appearer 1,"

AND

____________________________________ a ☐ single ☐ married ☐ widowed ☐ divorced (circle one) person, of the full age of majority, domiciled in and a resident of the Parish of ________________________, State of Louisiana, whose permanent mailing address is ____, and who declares unto me that he/she ☐ has never been married / ☐ has been married but once, to ____________________________________, from whom he/she was divorced in _________________ Parish, on _____________________, herein "Appearer 2,"

who declared unto me:

That they are the owners of interment rights in indivision in the Cemetery spaces described below herein, "Interment Rights":

Building/Location	**Section**	**Row/Unit**	**Space No(s).**

herein "Space 1" and

Building/Location	**Section**	**Row/Unit**	**Space No(s).**

herein "Space 2,"

APPEARERS declare that they no longer wish to remain owners in indivision and hereby partition the property as follows:

APPEARER 1 hereby transfers all interest, rights, title, and claims he/she has to SPACE 1 to APPEARER 2 in full ownership.

APPEARER 2 hereby transfers all interest, rights, title, and claims he/she has to SPACE 2 to APPEARER 1 in full ownership.

This Act of Partition is made without any warranties as to title, fitness for purpose, redhibition, or any other warranties and shall be binding on APPEARERS, their successors, heirs, and assigns, forever.

The parties acknowledge that this item was omitted from the community property partition between them recorded at ________________________________, and this transaction is a further partition of the former community between the parties, and the parties reiterate the terms therein, including waivers of right of rescission or dissolution, waiver of vendors liens, and further certify that the above described property is not encumbered and has not been alienated. The parties intend that this transfer shall be treated as a non-taxable transfer.

THUS, DONE, SIGNED, AND PASSED on the day and date first above mentioned, in the presence of the undersigned competent witnesses, who hereunto sign their names with the said appearers and me, Notary, after due reading of the whole.

WITNESSES:	**APPEARERS:**
______________________________	______________________________
Signature of Witness	Signature of Appearer 1
______________________________	______________________, APPEARER 1
Printed Name of Witness	Printed Name of Appearer 1
______________________________	______________________________
Signature of Witness	Signature of Appearer 2
______________________________	______________________, APPEARER 2
Printed Name of Witness	Printed Name of Appearer 2

____
Signature of Notary

Printed Notary Name: ______________________________

Notary ID or Bar Roll No.: ______________

My Commission is for Life

FORM 2.11

ACT OF EXCHANGE OF INTERMENT RIGHTS

FORM: 🚫 **NO NOTARIZATION REQUIRED**

FORM REQUIREMENTS: An Act of Exchange of interment rights among parties has the effect of conveying each party's interest. Under **La. C.C. arts. 1833 and 1839**, such acts may be executed as acts under private signature. Although real rights are being exchanged, it is not a real right in the property itself and so no notarization is required. Because of the importance of verification of parties, a notarization block is included on this document as notarization is preferred.

PURPOSE: Exchanges burial rights in spaces between parties when there is no act of sale or donation.

PURPOSE: Divides jointly owned interment rights among co-owners or heirs.

CITATION: La. C.C. art. 2660 – Of Exchange
"Exchange is a contract whereby each party transfers to the other the ownership of a thing other than money. Ownership of the things exchanged is transferred between the parties as soon as there is agreement on the things, even though none of the things have been delivered."

DESCRIPTION: Executed among heirs or multiple owners who wish to exchange the burial rights they have in their location with the burial rights in another location.

*** See Appendix for various forms of appearance clauses that can be used.**

ACT OF EXCHANGE OF CEMETERY INTERMENT RIGHTS

STATE OF LOUISIANA
PARISH OF ______________________________

BEFORE ME, the undersigned notary, duly commissioned and qualified in the state and parish aforesaid, PERSONALLY CAME and appeared:

_______________________________________, being of the full age of majority, residing at

____ "EXCHANGER 1"

AND

_______________________________________, being of the full age of majority, residing at

____ "EXCHANGER 2"

WHEREAS EXCHANGER 1 is the listed owner of interment rights in a certain burial crypt(s)/lot(s) described in the books of ___________________________ Cemetery as:

Building/Location	**Section**	**Row/Unit**	**Space No(s).**

hereinafter "Space A" AND

WHEREAS EXCHANGER 2 is the listed owner of interment rights in a certain burial crypt(s)/lot(s) described in the books of ____________________________Cemetery as:

Building/Location	**Section**	**Row/Unit**	**Space No(s).**

hereinafter "Space B",

NOW, THEREFORE, for and in consideration of the mutual covenants and agreements herein contained, the parties do hereby agree as follows:

5. **Transfer by EXCHANGER 1:** EXCHANGER 1 does hereby transfer, assign, and convey unto EXCHANGER 2 all of his right, title, and interest in and to SPACE A, together with all rights of interment and privileges appurtenant thereto.
6. **Transfer by EXCHANGER 2:** EXCHANGER 2 does hereby transfer, assign, and convey unto EXCHANGER 1 all of her right, title, and interest in and to SPACE B, together with all rights of interment and privileges appurtenant thereto.

7. **Even Exchange:** The parties expressly declare that this is an even exchange, that the interment rights described herein are considered by the parties to be of equal value, and that neither party owes nor shall owe any additional payment, reimbursement, or balancing sum.
8. **Nature of Rights:** The parties acknowledge that cemetery spaces constitute rights of interment only and do not convey ownership of the land itself.
9. **"As Is" Condition:** The exchange is made "AS IS" and without warranty of any kind, either express or implied, except as to authority and title.
10. **Binding Effect:** This agreement shall be binding upon and inure to the benefit of the parties hereto, their heirs, successors, and assigns.
11. **Acknowledgment of Cemetery Management**: Both EXCHANGER 1 and EXCHANGER 2 acknowledge that the CEMETERY has given consent for this conveyance. The transfer may require completing additional paperwork with the CEMETERY and paying transfer fees. This conveyance shall not have any binding effect until recorded by the CEMETERY in its official records.

The masculine pronoun used herein shall include the feminine; the singular shall include the plural, and vice versa.

THUS DONE, SIGNED AND PASSED on the _____ day of _________________, 20____, in ___________________, Louisiana, in the presence of me, the undersigned Notary Public, the undersigned competent witnesses who have signed their names together with the appearing party and me, after due reading of the whole.

EXCHANGER 1	EXCHANGER 2
______________________________	______________________________
Signature of Exchanger 1	Signature of Exchanger 2
______________________________	______________________________
Printed Name of Exchanger 1	Printed Name of Exchanger 2

____
Signature of Notary

Printed Notary Name: ______________________________

Notary ID or Bar Roll No.: _______________

My Commission is for Life

FORM 2.12

DATION EN PAIEMENT OF CEMETERY SPACE

FORM: ✎ **AUTHENTIC FORM REQUIRED**

FORM REQUIREMENTS: A *dation en paiement* (giving in payment) is a conveyance made in satisfaction of a debt and falls within the requirements of **La. C.C. arts. 1833 and 1839.** It must be executed before a **notary public and two witnesses.** The authentic act verifies the debtor's intent to transfer ownership or interment rights, ensures the creditor's acceptance, and allows the document to be recorded in the cemetery's or parish conveyance records as a valid satisfaction of obligation.

PURPOSE: Allows an owner to transfer cemetery spaces to satisfy an outstanding debt owed to the cemetery.

CITATION: La. C.C. art. 2655 – Dation en Paiement
"Dation en paiement is a contract whereby a debtor gives a thing to the creditor who accepts it in payment of a sum that is due."

DESCRIPTION: Used when a purchaser's account is delinquent. The Cemetery Authority accepts the space back in settlement of the unpaid balance, ending the obligation.

*** See Appendix for various forms of appearance clauses that can be used.**

DATION EN PAIEMENT OF CEMETERY SPACE

STATE OF LOUISIANA
PARISH OF ____________________________

BE IT KNOWN, that on this ____ day of _________________, 20_____, BEFORE ME, the undersigned Notary Public, duly commissioned and qualified in and for the Parish and State aforesaid, PERSONALLY CAME AND APPEARED:

_______________________________________ (xxx-xx-______), a ☐ single ☐ married ☐ widowed ☐ divorced (check one) person, of the full age of majority, domiciled in and a resident of the Parish of __________________________, State of Louisiana, whose permanent mailing address is ______________________________________, and who declares unto me that he/she ☐ has never been married / ☐ has been married but once, to ____________________________________, from whom he/she was divorced in _______________ Parish, on __________________, hereinafter "Debtor" or "Appearer,"

who declared that he/she is justly indebted unto:

____________________Cemetery a Louisiana corporation duly organized and existing under the laws of the State of Louisiana, domiciled in the Parish of __________________, State of Louisiana, having its principal place of business at ____, herein represented by ______________________________________, whose mailing address is ____, who declared that he/she is the duly authorized ☐ President ☐ Executive Director ☐ Authorized Officer/Agent of said corporation, and is duly empowered by appropriate corporate resolution to appear herein and to execute this act of dation en paiement on behalf of said corporation, herein "Creditor " or "Cemetery Authority"),

and that DEBTOR, being desirous of satisfying said indebtedness, does hereby declare that, in accordance with **Louisiana Civil Code Article 2655 et seq.**, he/she does make, execute, and deliver unto CREDITOR this DATION EN PAIEMENT, transferring and conveying, with full warranty of title, unto CREDITOR, the following described rights of interment:

One (1) cemetery interment right in a certain space located in __________________ Cemetery, situated in the Parish of ___________________, State of Louisiana, and more particularly described as follows:

Building/Location	**Section**	**Row/Unit**	**Space No(s).**

Together with all rights of interment, improvements, and appurtenances thereto belonging, subject to all rules, regulations, and restrictions of the Cemetery, and all provisions of **La. R.S Title 8.**

This transfer is made in full and complete satisfaction of the aforesaid indebtedness in the amount of ________________________________ ($__________________) Dollars, which the CREDITOR hereby acknowledges as fully paid, satisfied, and extinguished by this dation en paiement.

The DEBTOR warrants that he/she is the lawful holder of the interment rights described herein, that said rights are free of all liens and encumbrances, and that no prior interments have been made therein, except as follows: ____.

The CEMETERY AUTHORITY acknowledges receipt of all necessary documentation and accepts the transfer subject to its rules, regulations, and applicable law.

The CREDITOR/CEMETERY AUTHORITY agrees to hold the DEBTOR harmless from any further claim related to the satisfied debt described herein.

THUS, DONE, SIGNED, AND PASSED on the day and date first above mentioned, in the presence of the undersigned competent witnesses, who hereunto sign their names with the said appearers and me, Notary, after due reading of the whole.

WITNESSES:	**DEBTOR:**
______________________________	______________________________
Signature of Witness	Signature of Debtor
______________________________	______________________________
Printed Name of Witness	Printed Name of Debtor
	CREDITOR:
______________________________	______________________________
Signature of Witness	Signature of Creditor
______________________________	______________________________
Printed Name of Witness	Printed Name of Creditor

____

Signature of Notary

Printed Notary Name: ______________________________

Notary ID or Bar Roll No.: _______________

My Commission is for Life

FORM 2.13

PROMISSORY NOTE FOR CEMETERY INTERMENT RIGHTS

FORM: 🚫 **NO NOTARIZATION REQUIRED**

FORM REQUIREMENTS: promissory note is valid and enforceable under **private signature** in Louisiana in accordance with **La. C.C. art. 1837**. The note evidences a debt obligation between the purchaser and the Cemetery Authority. Notarization is optional but may be used for convenience in evidentiary matters or if the note is to be attached to an authentic act of sale or recorded as part of a lien file.

PURPOSE: Documents the purchaser's obligation to pay remaining balances under installment terms.

CITATION: **La. R.S. 8:454(B) – Credit Sales and Trust Deposits**
"Cemetery authorities may extend credit for the purchase of interment spaces provided that all trust fund deposits required by this Title are made from the proceeds."

DESCRIPTION: Used when the cemetery finances a sale. The document outlines the payment schedule, interest rates, and default provisions. Filed with sales contract to ensure trust deposits are funded adequately from each installment.

Note: Under **Louisiana law** (and general contract principles), a **promissory note** is a *unilateral promise to pay*— meaning **only the borrower (the obligor)** must sign it for it to be valid and enforceable. The **lender (the obligee)** does **not** need to sign the note, because:

1. **The borrower's signature** constitutes the promise to pay the lender a specific sum under specific terms.
2. **Delivery and acceptance** of the note (i.e., the lender providing the interment rights or financing) serve as consideration for the transaction.
3. If the lender signs, it doesn't invalidate the document, but it's unnecessary—and often avoided to keep the instrument clearly the borrower's obligation.

PROMISSORY NOTE FOR CEMETERY INTERMENT RIGHTS

Date: ____________________________ Note No.: ________________________

FOR VALUE RECEIVED, I, ____ (Borrower's full legal name, last four digits of SSN: xxx-xx-______), a ☐ single ☐ married ☐ widowed individual, domiciled in and a resident of ____________________ Parish, Louisiana, whose mailing address is ____,

PROMISES TO PAY to the order of:

____________________ Cemetery, a Louisiana ☐ nonprofit corporation ☐ other: ______________________, domiciled in ____________________ Parish, Louisiana, whose mailing address is ____, the principal sum of _________________________________ ($____________________) Dollars, together with interest thereon at the rate of _____ % per annum from the date hereof until paid in full, in lawful money of the United States, at the office of the Cemetery Authority or at such other place as the holder may designate in writing.

The Borrower agrees to pay this Note as follows:

Principal and interest payable in ____ monthly installments of $ _________ each, beginning on the ____ day of _________, 20_____, and continuing on the same day of each successive month thereafter until _________, 20_____, or until the indebtedness is paid in full.

If any installment remains unpaid more than ____ days after its due date, a late fee of $ ________ or _____ % of the installment amount (whichever is greater) shall be added.

Borrower may prepay this Note, in whole or in part, at any time without penalty. Any partial prepayment shall first be applied to accrued interest, then to principal.

If Borrower fails to make any payment when due or otherwise breaches any term hereof, the entire unpaid balance, at the option of the holder, shall become immediately due and payable without notice or demand. Upon default, interest shall accrue at the rate of _____ % per annum or the maximum rate permitted by law.

This Note is issued in connection with the purchase of the following rights of interment in the space(s) designated in the books of ____________ Cemetery as:

Building/Location	**Section**	**Row/Unit**	**Space No(s).**

The Cemetery Authority retains a vendor's lien and privilege upon the described cemetery space(s) until payment is made in full, as provided by **La. R.S. 8:308 et seq**. In the event of default, the Cemetery Authority may cancel the purchase agreement and retain all payments made as liquidated damages, subject to the provisions of Louisiana law.

Borrower agrees to pay all reasonable attorney fees and costs of collection if this Note is placed in the hands of an attorney for collection, whether or not suit is filed.

Borrower and all endorsers, sureties, and guarantors hereby waive presentment, demand, protest, and notice of non-payment and consent to extensions without notice.

This Note shall be governed by and construed in accordance with the laws of the State of Louisiana.

IN WITNESS WHEREOF, I have executed this Note on the date first above written.

WITNESSES:

____
Signature of Witness

____
Printed Name of Witness

____
Signature of Witness

____
Printed Name of Witness

BORROWER(S):

____
Signature of Borrower

____
Printed Name of Borrower

____
Signature of Co-Borrower

____
Printed Name of Co-Borrower

NOTARIAL ACKNOWLEDGMENT (Optional)

STATE OF LOUISIANA
PARISH OF ____________________

On this _____ day of _______________, 20_____, before me, the undersigned Notary Public, personally appeared ____, who declared and acknowledged that they executed the foregoing Promissory Note as their free and voluntary act for the purposes therein stated.

____
Signature of Notary

Printed Notary Name: ______________________________
Notary ID or Bar Roll No.: _______________
My Commission is for Life

FORM 2.14

TRANSFER AND ASSIGNMENT OF INTERMENT RIGHTS (EXCHANGE AGREEMENT)

FORM: 🚫 **NO NOTARIZATION REQUIRED**

FORM REQUIREMENTS: NO NOTATIZATION REQUIRED.
When executed between a purchaser and the Cemetery Authority, it is an **administrative transaction** handled under private signature but is considered an Authentic Act under **La. R.S 8:812**. The cemetery's acknowledgment and internal record entry complete the exchange.

PURPOSE: Enables an owner to exchange one interment space for another within the same cemetery, with options for even trade, upgrade, or refund.

CITATION: La. R.S. 8:801–806 – Transfer and Use of Interment Rights
"The right of interment is a transferable, limited right of use, subject to the rules and regulations of the Cemetery Authority and the provisions of this Title."

DESCRIPTION: Used when a family relocates burial plans or prefers a different space. The system records both the surrendered and replacement spaces, as well as any payment adjustments.

TRANSFER AND ASSIGNMENT OF INTERMENT RIGHTS (EXCHANGE AGREEMENT)

This Transfer and Assignment of Cemetery Interment Rights (Exchange Agreement), herein "Agreement," is made and entered into this _____ day of ______________, 20_____, by and between:

____

____

____ herein "Assignor," and

________________________________Cemetery

____

_______________________________________ herein "Cemetery Authority" or "Assignee."

RECITALS

WHEREAS, the ASSIGNOR is the lawful owner of the rights of interment in ____________________ Cemetery, located in the Parish of ___________________, Louisiana, designated in the books and records of said Cemetery as follows:

Building/Location	**Section**	**Row/Unit**	**Space No(s).**

WHEREAS the ASSIGNOR desires to transfer and assign all rights, title, and interest in the above-described cemetery space(s) to the ASSIGNEE in exchange for another interment space owned by the CEMETERY AUTHORITY; and

WHEREAS, both parties agree that this exchange may be an even exchange, an upgrade involving additional payment, or a downgrade involving a refund to the Assignor.

NOW, THEREFORE, in consideration of the mutual covenants and promises contained herein, the parties agree as follows:

TERMS AND CONDITIONS

1. **Transfer of Title:**
   The ASSIGNOR warrants that the cemetery space(s) described above are free of encumbrances and that the ASSIGNOR has full right to transfer and assign title to the ASSIGNEE.
2. **Assumption of Rights:**
   The ASSIGNEE accepts and assumes all rights, responsibilities, and obligations associated with the above cemetery space(s) upon execution of this Agreement.

3. **Exchange DESCRIPTION:**
The ASSIGNEE agrees to transfer and assign to the ASSIGNOR the following replacement interment rights in the following space(s):

Building/Location	**Section**	**Row/Unit**	**Space No(s).**

4. **Value Adjustment:**
The parties acknowledge that the exchange may involve one of the following conditions (check one):

☐ **Even Exchange:** No additional consideration is required by either party.

☐ **Upgrade:** The ASSIGNOR agrees to pay the CEMETERY AUTHORITY the sum of ____________________________ Dollars ($_____________) representing the difference in value between the exchanged spaces.

☐ **Downgrade:** The CEMETERY AUTHORITY agrees to ☐ refund ☐ credit the ASSIGNOR the sum of ____________________________ Dollars ($_____________) representing the difference in value between the exchanged spaces

All adjustments shall be settled in full at the time of execution of this Agreement.

5. **Effective Date:**
This Transfer and Assignment of Interment Rights shall become effective immediately upon execution by both parties and acceptance by the CEMETERY AUTHORITY.
6. **Acknowledgment of Cemetery Management:**
Both parties acknowledge that the cemetery management has been informed of this exchange and that approval has been granted, if required. Additional administrative forms may be completed to update official cemetery records.

IN WITNESS WHEREOF, the ASSIGNOR and ASSIGNEE have executed this Transfer and Assignment of Interment Rights (Exchange Agreement) as of the day and year first above written.

ASSIGNEE(S):

____
Signature of Authorized Representative

FOR _____________ CEMETERY, INC
.

By ________________________________
Printed Name of Authorized Representative

ASSIGNOR(S):

____
Signature of Assignor

____
Printed Name of Assignor

____
Signature of Assignor

____
Printed Name of Assignor

FORM 2.15

PURCHASER'S RIGHT OF CANCELLATION (THREE-BUSINESS-DAY OPTION)

FORM: 🚫 **NO NOTARIZATION REQUIRED**

FORM REQUIREMENTS: This form does **not require notarization.** It is a consumer notice executed under private signature and maintained in the cemetery's administrative file.

PURPOSE: Provides purchasers with a voluntary three-business-day period to cancel their cemetery purchase contract when the Cemetery Authority offers such a right.

CITATION: No statutory rescission period is required under Louisiana law.

EXPLANATION: Louisiana Revised Statutes Title 8 does not mandate a cancellation or rescission period for cemetery sales contracts. However, a Cemetery Authority may **voluntarily grant** such a right as a matter of consumer service or policy.

PURCHASER'S RIGHT OF CANCELLATION NOTICE

Contract No.: ____________________________ Date of Contract: ________________________

CEMETERY AUTHORITY:

Name: ____

Address: ____

City/Parish/State: _______________________________

Phone: ________________________ Email: _________________________________

PURCHASER:

Name: ____

Address: ____

City/State/ZIP: ____

YOUR RIGHT TO CANCEL

You, the PURCHASER, may cancel this Cemetery Purchase Agreement **without penalty or obligation** by delivering or mailing written notice to the CEMETERY AUTHORITY at the address above **no later than midnight of the third (3rd) business day** after the date the Agreement was executed.

If you cancel within that time, you will receive a **full refund of all payments made**, minus only the costs expressly authorized by law and itemized in your contract.

To cancel, you must give written notice stating that you wish to cancel your Cemetery Purchase Agreement. You may deliver it in person or send it by **certified or registered mail** to the CEMETERY AUTHORITY at the address listed above.

If you send your cancellation notice by mail, the postmark date will control whether your cancellation is timely.

NOTICE OF CANCELLATION

Date: ______________________

I hereby cancel my Cemetery Purchase Agreement, Contract No. _________________, executed on this ______ day of ___________________, 20_____.

____
Purchaser Signature

____
Printed Name

Address: ____

City/State/ZIP: _____________________________________

ACKNOWLEDGMENT OF RECEIPT

The undersigned Purchaser acknowledges receipt of **a copy** of this **Right of Cancellation Notice** at the time of signing the Cemetery Purchase Agreement.

Purchaser: ____ Date: ____________

Cemetery Representative: ___________________________ Date: ____________

FORM 2.16

PURCHASER'S NOTICE: NO STATUTORY CANCELLATION PERIOD

FORM: 🚫 **NO NOTARIZATION REQUIRED**

FORM REQUIREMENTS: This form does **not require notarization.** It is an informational disclosure signed by the purchaser under private signature to acknowledge receipt of the cemetery's policy.

PURPOSE: Clarifies that Louisiana law does not require a statutory rescission period for cemetery interment rights purchases but allows the cemetery to establish one voluntarily.

CITATION: **No statutory cancellation period is required by La. R.S. Title 8.**

EXPLANATION: Louisiana law does not grant purchasers of cemetery interment rights an automatic right to cancel after they have signed the contract. This notice ensures consumers are informed that cancellations or refunds are governed solely by the cemetery's published policies and contract terms.

PURCHASER'S NOTICE

Date of Contract: ____________________________

Contract No.: ________________________________

Louisiana law does not require a cancellation or rescission period for cemetery interment rights contracts. This cemetery's policy regarding cancellations, transfers, or refunds is stated in its Rules and Regulations and on your purchase agreement. Please review those terms carefully before signing.

Signature of Purchaser _________________________________ Date _____________

Acknowledged by Cemetery Authority ________________________ Date _____________

FORM 2.17

INTERMENT ORDER

FORM: 🚫 **NO NOTARIZATION REQUIRED**

FORM REQUIREMENTS: It is an operational authorization signed by the person with the right of disposition and accepted by the Cemetery Authority.

PURPOSE: Authorizes burial of the named deceased in the designated space.

CITATION: La. R.S. 8:803(C) – Proof of Ownership Before Interment
"A Cemetery Authority shall not permit an interment until proof of ownership or written consent of all owners of record has been provided."

DESCRIPTION: Completed by the person with the interment authority. Identifies decedent, date, and location of interment, and provides official record authorization.

INTERMENT ORDER

I/We, ____, Grantor(s), owning interment rights in ___________________ Cemetery herein "Cemetery," do hereby authorize CEMETERY to inter the remains of _____________________________, herein "Decedent," in the following space(s) designated in the books of ___________ Cemetery as:

Building/Location	**Section**	**Row/Unit**	**Space No(s).**

in ___________________Cemetery, in the Parish of ___________________, State of Louisiana, according to the plat thereof, for burial purposes only and no other.

The undersigned hereby certifies they have the full legal authority to direct the Interment, Entombment, or Inurnment, including cremated remains of the above-named DECEDENT, and hereby authorizes CEMETERY to make disposition of the remains of DECEDENT as indicated. The undersigned hereby further certifies and represents that they are the owner(s) or authorized representative(s) of the owner(s) of the above-described Interment Rights and hereby authorize use of said Interment Rights for the Interment, Entombment, or Inurnment of the remains of the herein named DECEDENT.

GRANTOR(s) also authorize(s) CEMETERY to provide and install any plaques, markers, or monuments purchased on any separate agreements for the aforesaid DECEDENT without notice.

When cremated remains are presented to CEMETERY, the undersigned warrants and represents to the CEMETERY that they have the full authorization to deliver such cremated remains to CEMETERY and that the cremated remains are those and only those of the named DECEDENT.

The undersigned hereby agrees to indemnify and hold harmless the CEMETERY, its agents and employees from any and all Liability, including reasonable attorney's fees, and against any loss it or they may sustain in connection with the Interment, Entombment, or Inurnment authorized hereunder. The CEMETERY takes great care to avoid errors, but in the event an inadvertent error does occur, the CEMETERY shall have the right to correct any error in the Interment, Entombment, or Inurnment at its own expense, without any liability for such error.

Hereby ordered on this ____day of ____________, 20_______.

_________________________________ _________________________________

Grantor or Authorized Representative Grantor or Authorized Representative

FORM 2.18

DECLARATION OF INTERMENT LOCATION FOR BURIAL OF OWNER

FORM: 🚫 **NO NOTARIZATION REQUIRED**

FORM REQUIREMENTS: This form does **not require notarization** when filed with the cemetery. If intended for use in probate or succession proceedings, a notarial acknowledgment may be added for evidentiary purposes.

PURPOSE: Identifies which specific cemetery space the owner designates for his or her own future interment.

CITATION: La. R.S. 8:803 – Use of Interment Space
"The person having the right of interment in a cemetery space may determine who may be interred therein, and the Cemetery Authority shall permit interment in accordance with such written authorization."

DESCRIPTION: Executed by the owner to designate a personal burial location, ensuring clarity of intent. Filed in the cemetery's records to guide future burial arrangements and prevent family disputes.

DECLARATION OF INTERMENT LOCATION FOR BURIAL OF OWNER

STATE OF LOUISIANA
PARISH OF ____________________

BE IT KNOWN, that on this _____ day of _______________, 20_____, before me, the undersigned, personally came and appeared:

____, of the age of majority, domiciled in and a resident of ____________________ Parish, Louisiana, herein "Declarant,"

who declares as follows:

____ herein "Decedent" who died on or about ____________________________was the lawful owner of the following interment rights located within ____________________ Cemetery, situated in ____________________ Parish, Louisiana:

Building/Location	**Section**	**Row/Unit**	**Space No(s).**

The DECLARANT hereby designates and authorizes that the remains of the aforementioned DECEDENT shall be interred in the aforementioned space, owned by the DECEDENT.

This declaration is made to direct the CEMETERY AUTHORITY to the proper location for interment and to avoid any doubt or dispute concerning the placement of remains.

This declaration shall be binding upon the DECLARANT, their heirs, successors, and assigns, and may be relied upon by the CEMETERY AUTHORITY as sufficient written authorization for the interment in the space designated above.

The DECLARANT affirms that the statements contained herein are true and correct to the best of their knowledge and belief and are made voluntarily for cemetery record purposes.

DECLARANT:

____
Signature of Declarant

____
Printed Name of Declarant

FORM 2.19

CEMETERY INTERMENT RECORD

FORM: 🚫 **NO NOTARIZATION REQUIRED**

FORM REQUIREMENTS: It is an internal record prepared and certified by the Cemetery Authority.

PURPOSE: Creates a permanent record of each interment, including the decedent's name, date of burial, and precise grave or crypt location.

CITATION: La. R.S. 8:803(D) – Record of Interments
"Each Cemetery Authority shall maintain accurate records of every interment, including the name of the decedent, date of interment, and exact location."

DESCRIPTION: Completed by cemetery staff at the time of burial and retained permanently in the interment register to ensure compliance with Title 8 and facilitate genealogical and legal inquiries.

CEMETERY INTERMENT RECORD

Name of Deceased:		
Date of Birth:		
Date of Death:		
Date of Burial:		
Burial Type:		
LOCATION OF INTERMENT	Building:	
	Section:	
	Row/Unit:	
	Space No(s).:	
Funeral Home:		
Funeral Director:		
Contact Name:		
Contact Phone:		

I hereby certify that the above information is accurate to the best of my knowledge:

____

Signature of Authorized Representative

FORM 2.20

AFFIDAVIT OF LOST OR DESTROYED DEED / CERTIFICATE

FORM: **NOTARIZATION REQUIRED.**

FORM REQUIREMENTS: An affidavit under oath requires a **jurat** before a notary public verifying the affiant's sworn statement.

PURPOSE: Provides sworn proof that an original interment rights certificate was lost or destroyed to authorize a duplicate issuance.

CITATION: **La. R.S. 8:802(E) – Duplicate Certificates**
"Each Cemetery Authority shall keep records of all certificates of ownership and may issue a duplicate certificate upon satisfactory proof of loss or destruction."

DESCRIPTION: Typically executed before a notary by the recorded owner and maintained in the cemetery's files to document the reason for issuing a new ownership record.

AFFIDAVIT OF LOST OR DESTROYED DEED

STATE OF LOUISIANA
PARISH OF ___________________________

ON THIS DAY, the ______ day of __________________, 20 ____ before me, the undersigned Notary Public, PERSONALLY CAME AND APPEARED:

____ herein "Affiant," who, after being duly sworn, did say:

That AFFIANT is the lawful holder of interment rights in space(s) designated in the books of ____________________ Cemetery, in the Parish of ______________________________, Louisiana as:

Building/Location	**Section**	**Row/Unit**	**Space No(s).**

That the original Deed of Interment Rights has been:
☐ lost ☐ destroyed ☐ defaced and cannot be located.

That AFFIANT requests issuance of a **Duplicate Deed** and agrees to indemnify and hold harmless the CEMETERY AUTHORITY from any claim that may arise from the re-issuance of said certificate.

AFFIANT:

____
Signature of Affiant

____
Printed Name of Affiant

SWORN TO AND SUBSCRIBED before me on this ____ day of ______________, 20____

____
Signature of Notary

Printed Notary Name: ______________________________
Notary ID or Bar Roll No.: _______________
My Commission is for Life

FORM 2.21

TRANSFER AND ASSIGNMENT OF INTERMENT RIGHTS

FORM: 🚫 NO NOTARIZATION REQUIRED; 🖋 AUTHENTIC FORM VERSION PROVIDED

FORM REQUIREMENTS: A transfer of interment rights between private individuals must be in writing but need not be executed in authentic form. Under **La. C.C. art. 1839**, a transfer of immovable property, which includes an interment right, may be made by act under private signature, and it is valid between the parties from the time it is signed; however, it has effect against third persons only from the time it is filed for registry in the conveyance records of the parish where the cemetery is located. Although an authentic act is not required, acknowledgment before a notary under **La. C.C. art. 1836** is recommended to provide full evidentiary value and simplify recordation. Parties may also choose to execute the assignment as an authentic act before a notary and two witnesses, but this is optional. A copy of the executed instrument should be provided to the cemetery authority so that its internal ownership records can be updated in accordance with **La. R.S. 8:812(C).**

PURPOSE: Transfers burial rights from one private owner to another, with the Cemetery Authority's approval.

CITATION: La. R.S. 8:805(A) – Transfer or Assignment of Interment Rights
"An owner of interment rights may transfer or assign them by written instrument subject to the rules of the Cemetery Authority."

DESCRIPTION: Used when interment rights are sold to another person and filed with the cemetery, which issues an updated certificate of ownership to the assignee.

TRANSFER AND ASSIGNMENT OF CEMETERY RIGHTS
(Non-Authentic Form Version)

ON THIS______ day of __________________, 20______, the following did appear:

____

____

_____________________________________ herein "Assignor," and

____

____

_____________________________________ herein "Assignee."

RECITALS

WHEREAS the ASSIGNOR is the lawful owner/heir of interment rights in space(s) designated in the books of ____________________ Cemetery as:

Building/Location	**Section**	**Row/Unit**	**Space No(s).**

WHEREAS the ASSIGNOR desires to transfer and assign all rights, title, and interest in the above-described cemetery space(s) to the ASSIGNEES.

NOW, THEREFORE, for and in consideration of the Terms and Conditions below, the ASSIGNOR hereby transfers, conveys, and assigns all right, title, and interest in and to the above-described cemetery spaces(s) to the ASSIGNEE, their successors, and assigns, to have and hold forever.

TERMS AND CONDITIONS

1. **Transfer of Title:** The ASSIGNOR warrants that the cemetery space(s) described above are free from any encumbrances and that the ASSIGNOR has the full right to transfer and assign the title to the ASSIGNEE.
2. **Rules and Regulations Compliance:** ASSIGNEE agrees to be bound by and comply with Cemetery Rules and Regulations, as they may be supplemented and amended from time to time. The Rules and Regulations are binding not only upon the ASSIGNEE but on each person who derives or claims to derive rights through or by virtue of the ASSIGNEE.
3. **Assumption of Rights:** The ASSIGNEE assumes all rights, responsibilities, and obligations associated with the cemetery space(s) upon the execution of this Agreement.
4. **Payment:** The ASSIGNEE agrees to issue payment to ASSIGNOR in the sum of _______________ _________________Dollars ($___________) as full consideration for this transfer and assignment.

5. **Effective Date:** This Transfer and Assignment of Cemetery Space Title shall be effective immediately upon execution by both parties.

6. **Acknowledgment of Cemetery Management:** Both the ASSIGNOR and ASSIGNEE acknowledge that the cemetery management has given consent for the transfer of the above cemetery space(s). The transfer may require the completion of additional paperwork with the cemetery administration and payment of transfer fees.

EXECUTION

IN WITNESS WHEREOF, the ASSIGNORS and ASSIGNEES have executed this Transfer and Assignment of Cemetery Space Title as of the day and year first above written.

ASSIGNEE(S):	**ASSIGNOR(S):**
______________________________	______________________________
Signature of Assignee	Signature of Assignor
______________________________	______________________________
Printed Name of Assignee	Printed Name of Assignor
______________________________	______________________________
Signature of Assignee	Signature of Assignor
______________________________	______________________________
Printed Name of Assignee	Printed Name of Assignor

TRANSFER AND ASSIGNMENT OF CEMETERY RIGHTS
(Authentic Form Version)

STATE OF LOUISIANA
PARISH OF ________________

ON THIS DAY, the ______ day of ________________, 20 _____ before me, the undersigned Notary Public, PERSONALLY CAME AND APPEARED:

____
____
____________________________________ herein "Assignor," and

____
____
____________________________________ herein "Assignee."

WHEREAS the ASSIGNOR is the lawful owner/heir of interment rights in space(s) designated in the books of ___________________ Cemetery as:

Building/Location	**Section**	**Row/Unit**	**Space No(s).**

WHEREAS the ASSIGNOR desires to transfer and assign all rights, title, and interest in the above-described cemetery space(s) to the ASSIGNEES.

NOW, THEREFORE, for and in consideration of the Terms and Conditions below, the ASSIGNOR hereby transfers, conveys, and assigns all right, title, and interest in and to the above-described cemetery spaces(s) to the ASSIGNEE, their successors, and assigns, to have and hold forever.

TERMS AND CONDITIONS

1. **Transfer of Title:** The ASSIGNOR warrants that the cemetery space(s) described above are free from any encumbrances and that the ASSIGNOR has the full right to transfer and assign the title to the ASSIGNEE.

2. **Rules and Regulations Compliance:** ASSIGNEE agrees to be bound by and comply with Cemetery Rules and Regulations, as they may be supplemented and amended from time to time. The Rules and Regulations are binding not only upon the ASSIGNEE but on each person who derives or claims to derive rights through or by virtue of the ASSIGNEE.

3. **Assumption of Rights:** The ASSIGNEE assumes all rights, responsibilities, and obligations associated with the cemetery space(s) upon the execution of this Agreement.

4. **Payment:** The ASSIGNEE agrees to issue payment to ASSIGNOR in the sum of _______________ _________________Dollars ($___________) as full consideration for this transfer and assignment.

5. **Effective Date:** This Transfer and Assignment of Cemetery Space Title shall be effective

immediately upon execution by both parties.

6. **Acknowledgment of Cemetery Management:** Both the ASSIGNOR and ASSIGNEE acknowledge that the cemetery management has given consent for the transfer of the above cemetery space(s). The transfer may require the completion of additional paperwork with the cemetery administration and payment of transfer fees.

EXECUTION

THUS, DONE AND SIGNED in the Parish and State aforesaid, on the day, month, and year first above written, in the presence of the undersigned competent witnesses and Notary Public, after due reading of the whole.

WITNESSES

____
Signature of Witness

____
Printed Name of Witness

____
Signature of Witness

____
Printed Name of Witness

ASSIGNOR(S):

____
Signature of Assignor

____
Printed Name of Assignor

____
Signature of Assignor

____
Printed Name of Assignor

ASSIGNEE(S):

____
Signature of Assignee

____
Printed Name of Assignee

____
Signature of Assignee

____
Printed Name of Assignee

____
Signature of Notary

Printed Notary Name: ________________________________

Notary ID or Bar Roll No.: ________________

My Commission is for Life

FORM 2.22

NOTICE OF TRANSFER OR SALE TO CEMETERY AUTHORITY

FORM: 🚫 **NO NOTARIZATION REQUIRED**

FORM REQUIREMENTS: This form does **not require notarization.** It merely serves as written notice for the cemetery's records.

PURPOSE: Notifies the cemetery of a completed transfer so official records may be updated before any future interments occur.

CITATION: La. R.S. 8:803(C) – Proof of Ownership Before Interment
"A Cemetery Authority shall not permit an interment until proof of ownership or written consent of all owners of record has been provided."

DESCRIPTION: Filed with the cemetery immediately after a sale or transfer. Ensures that ownership records reflect the proper party entitled to authorize future burials.

NOTICE OF TRANSFER OR SALE OF INTERMENT RIGHTS

To: ____ (Cemetery Authority)
From: ____ (Transferor)
Date: ______________________

Please be advised that interment rights in the following space(s) have been sold or transferred:

Building/Location	**Section**	**Row/Unit**	**Space No(s).**

to ______________________________ (Transferee)

of ____
____ (Address)

Attached is a copy of the executed Assignment or Transfer Agreement for your records. TRANSFEROR hereby respectfully requests that CEMETERY AUTHORITY ratify this Transfer and record such in its official record.

Respectfully submitted,

____
Signature of Transferor

____
Printed Name of Transferor

____
Date

FORM 2.23

AFFIDAVIT OF LOST PROOF OF PURCHASE OF A BURIAL SPACE

FORM: 🖉 **NOTARIZATION REQUIRED**

FORM REQUIREMENTS: This form **must be notarized** because it is an affidavit made under oath. A **jurat** (sworn statement) is required; an acknowledgment alone is insufficient.

PURPOSE: Affirms ownership of a burial space when the original certificate, deed, or purchase receipt has been lost.

CITATION: La. R.S. 8:802(E) – Duplicate Certificates
"Each Cemetery Authority shall keep records of all certificates of ownership and may issue a duplicate certificate upon satisfactory proof of loss or destruction."

DESCRIPTION: Signed by the purchaser and accepted by the cemetery as evidence of purchase. Allows the Cemetery Authority to issue a replacement certificate to maintain proper ownership documentation.

AFFIDAVIT OF LOST PROOF OF PURCHASE OF A BURIAL SPACE

STATE OF LOUISIANA
PARISH OF ____________________________

BEFORE ME, the undersigned Notary Public, duly commissioned and qualified in and for the Parish and State aforesaid, PERSONALLY CAME AND APPEARED:

Affiant Name: ____
Address: ____
City/State/ZIP: ____herein "Affiant,"

who, after being duly sworn, did depose and say:

That AFFIANT is (check one):
☐ The original purchaser of the burial space described herein.
☐ The heir, successor, or authorized representative of the original purchaser.

That the interment right in question is located within _________________________ Cemetery, herein "Cemetery Authority," and designated in the books of ____________________ Cemetery as:

Building/Location	**Section**	**Row/Unit**	**Space No(s).**

and that said space was originally purchased on or about the ____day of _________________, _______, from the CEMETERY AUTHORITY.

That AFFIANT has **lost, misplaced, or is otherwise unable to locate the original proof of purchase** (such as the original burial deed, certificate of interment right, or receipt).

Despite diligent search, said document **cannot now be found**, and it is not in the possession of any other person to the best of AFFIANT'S knowledge and belief.

That AFFIANT has **not transferred, assigned, or encumbered** said interment right in any way, and that affiant remains the lawful holder or successor to the burial space described above.

AFFIANT understands that any false statement made in this affidavit may subject the AFFIANT to criminal or civil penalties under Louisiana law.

AFFIANT respectfully requests that the CEMETERY AUTHORITY issue a **duplicate certificate of purchase or proof of ownership** in the same manner as the original, reflecting AFFIANT'S lawful entitlement to the burial space.

AFFIANT agrees to **indemnify and hold harmless** the Cemetery Authority, its officers, successors, and assigns from any and all claims, losses, or expenses arising from the issuance of a duplicate proof of purchase, should the original document later be found or presented by another party.

AFFIANT:

____
Signature of Affiant

____
Printed Name of Affiant

____
Date

SWORN TO AND SUBSCRIBED before me on
this ____ day of ______________, 20____

____
Signature of Notary

Printed Notary Name: ______________________________
Notary ID or Bar Roll No.: _______________
My Commission is for Life

FORM 2.24

CANCELLATION AND REFUND REQUEST FORM

FORM: 🚫 **NO NOTARIZATION REQUIRED**

FORM REQUIREMENTS: This form does **not require notarization.** It is an administrative request between the purchaser and the Cemetery Authority, valid under private signature.

PURPOSE

Allows a purchaser to request cancellation of a cemetery purchase and a refund of any payments made, in accordance with the cemetery's own policies or a voluntarily granted rescission period.

CITATION: No specific statutory rescission requirement under Title 8; voluntary refunds permitted under Louisiana Consumer Protection Law (**La. R.S. 51:1401 et seq.**).

QUOTED AUTHORITY (CONSUMER PROTECTION ACT): "Unfair or deceptive acts or practices in the conduct of any trade or commerce are hereby declared unlawful." – **La. R.S. 51:1405(A)**

EXPLANATION: Louisiana cemetery law (Title 8) does **not** require a mandatory rescission period or refund right. However, a Cemetery Authority may provide one as a matter of policy or consumer courtesy. If a refund or cancellation policy is offered, this form provides written documentation of the purchaser's request and the cemetery's response, ensuring transparency and compliance with record-keeping requirements.

CANCELLATION AND REFUND REQUEST

To: ____ herein "Cemetery Authority"

From: ____ herein "Purchaser"
Address: ____
Phone/Email: _______________________________________

I hereby exercise my right to cancel my **Cemetery Space Purchase Agreement** dated ______________________ and request a refund of all amounts paid, less authorized costs.

Interment Rights Description:

Building/Location	**Section**	**Row/Unit**	**Space No(s).**

Executed this _______ day of ___________________, 20_____.

____
Signature of Purchaser

____
Printed Name of Purchaser

FORM 2.25

ACT OF DONATION OF CEMETERY SPACE

FORM: ✎ **AUTHENTIC FORM REQUIRED**

FORM REQUIREMENTS: Under **La. C.C. arts. 1468 and 1839**, a donation *inter vivos* requires execution before a notary public and two witnesses to be valid and recordable. Acceptance by the Donee may be done at a separate time and does not require notarization.

PURPOSE: Conveys interment rights to another individual or entity as a gratuitous gift.

CITATION: La. C.C. art. 1468 – Donation *Inter Vivos* Defined
"A donation *inter vivos* is a contract by which a person gratuitously divests himself, at present and irrevocably, of a thing in favor of another who accepts it."

DESCRIPTION: Executed in writing by the donor and accepted by the donee. The cemetery files the act in its records and issues a new ownership certificate to the recipient.

*** See Appendix for various forms of appearance clauses that can be used.**

ACT OF DONATION

STATE OF LOUISIANA
PARISH OF ____________________________

BE IT KNOWN that on this ______day of ___________, 20_____, before me, the undersigned Notary Public, duly commissioned in and for the Parish and state aforesaid, and in the presence of the witnesses herein named and undersigned PERSONALLY, CAME AND APPEARED:

_______________________________________ a ☐ single ☐ married ☐ widowed ☐ divorced (circle one) person, of the full age of majority, domiciled in and a resident of the Parish of _________________________, State of Louisiana, whose permanent mailing address is ____, and who declares unto me that he/she ☐ has never been married / ☐ has been married but once, to _____________________________________, from whom he/she was divorced in _________________ Parish, on _____________________, herein "Donor,"

who, after being duly sworn by me, declared that in consideration of the love and affection which DONOR has and bears for:

_______________________________________ a ☐ single ☐ married ☐ widowed ☐ divorced (circle one) person, of the full age of majority, domiciled in and a resident of the Parish of _________________________, State of Louisiana, whose permanent mailing address is____, and who declares unto me that he/she ☐ has never been married / ☐ has been married but once, to _____________________________________, from whom he/she was divorced in _________________ Parish, on _____________________, herein "Donee,"

,
DONOR does hereby give, convey, transfer, and donate all his title, interest, and rights of interment described in the books of ___________________ Cemetery as:

Building/Location	**Section**	**Row/Unit**	**Space No(s).**

DONOR declares that he intends to make an irrevocable donation inter vivos to DONEE. The right of interment donated herein shall be the separate property of DONEE. DONEE, personally accepting this donation in writing, with said donation complete upon signing acceptance, does by her signature accept with gratitude, each for himself/herself, and her successors and assigns.

DONOR declares that this conveyance has been consented to by ____________________ Cemetery and shall not have effect until accepted and entered into the official records of the Cemetery. This conveyance is made in accordance with and subject to the laws of the State of Louisiana now or herein existing governing cemeteries and the descent of right in cemetery lots, burial plots, or entombment or inurnment space or the right to burial, entombment, or inurnment therein; and in accordance with and subject to the rules and regulations of ____________________ Cemetery, Inc. now or herein existing or as decided or interpreted by the Management of ____________________ Cemetery and upon payment of all applicable fees as determined by the Cemetery, including all interment and memorial fees.

THUS, DONE AND SIGNED on the day and date first above mentioned, in the presence of the undersigned competent witnesses, who hereunto sign their names with the said appearers and me, Notary, after due reading of the whole.

WITNESSES:

____
Signature of Witness

____
Printed Name of Witness

____
Signature of Witness

____
Printed Name of Witness

DONOR:

____
Signature of Donor

______________________________, DONOR
Printed Name of Donor

____
Signature of Notary

Printed Notary Name: ______________________________
Notary ID or Bar Roll No.: ______________
My Commission is for Life

ACCEPTANCE:

COMES NOW the DONEE, ______________________, who by this signature hereby acknowledges that he/she has read the foregoing and freely and fully accepts the donation as stated in this instrument.

____
Signature of Donee

_________________________, DONEE
Printed Name of Donee

____
Date

FORM 2.26

AFFIDAVIT OF HEIRSHIP OF CEMETERY SPACE (BY DISINTERESTED PARTY)

FORM: ✎ **NOTARIZATION REQUIRED**

FORM REQUIREMENTS: The notary must complete a jurat confirming that the affiant appeared and swore to the facts contained in the document.

PURPOSE: Establishes the legal heirs to a burial space when the original owner died intestate.

CITATION: La. R.S. 8:804
"In the absence of a formal judgment of possession in the succession of the record owner of a cemetery space or right of interment, an affidavit by a disinterested but informed person of the facts setting forth the fact of the death of the record owner and identifying the spouse and legal heirs of the decedent shall be complete and sufficient authorization for a cemetery authority to permit the use of any unoccupied portion of a cemetery space by the person or persons entitled to the use thereof.."

DESCRIPTION: Completed by a disinterested, but informed person familiar with the decedent's family and used to identify rightful heirs for cemetery records without requiring formal probate.

AFFIDAVIT OF HEIRSHIP OF CEMETERY SPACE BY INFORMED BUT DISINTERESTED PARTY

STATE OF LOUISIANA
PARISH OF ___________________________

BEFORE ME, the undersigned Notary Public, duly commissioned and qualified in and for the Parish and State aforesaid, PERSONALLY CAME AND APPEARED:

Affiant Name: ____
Address: ____
City/State/ZIP: ____
Phone: ____

who, being of the age of majority and after first being duly sworn, did depose and say:

That AFFIANT is personally acquainted with the family and history of the deceased person named below, and makes this affidavit **as a disinterested person**, having **no present or future financial or ownership interest** in the burial space described herein.

That the deceased person whose burial space ownership is in question is:

Name of Deceased Owner: ____
Date of Death: ___________________________
Parish of Death: ___________________________

and that said person was, to the best of AFFIANT'S knowledge, the **lawful owner or purchaser of the following burial space(s)** in ____________________ Cemetery and that the lawful owner has never sold or transferred said burial rights to any other party.

Building/Location	**Section**	**Row/Unit**	**Space No(s).**

That the said deceased left surviving, to the best of AFFIANT'S knowledge and belief, the following heirs at law, whose names, relationships, and last known addresses are as follows:

Name	Relationship to Deceased	Address	Living/Deceased
			☐ Living ☐ Deceased
			☐ Living ☐ Deceased
			☐ Living ☐ Deceased
			☐ Living ☐ Deceased
			☐ Living ☐ Deceased

That AFFIANT has known the deceased and his/her family for approximately ______ years and is familiar with their relationships and family circumstances.

To the best of AFFIANT'S knowledge, no formal succession has been opened for the deceased, and no conflicting claim to the burial space has been made.

This affidavit is made for the purpose of assisting the CEMETERY AUTHORITY in determining lawful heirship and the persons entitled to the rights of interment and control of the above-described burial space, in accordance with **La. R.S. 8:801 – 806**.

AFFIANT further declares that they are not an heir, legatee, creditor, or other interested party in the estate of the deceased, and that this affidavit is made voluntarily and without request for compensation or benefit.

AFFIANT:

____

Signature of Affiant

____

Printed Name of Affiant

____

Date

SWORN TO AND SUBSCRIBED before me on
this ____ day of ______________, 20____

____

Signature of Notary

Printed Notary Name: ______________________________

Notary ID or Bar Roll No.: ______________

My Commission is for Life

FORM 2.27

WAIVER OF INTERMENT RIGHTS BY FAMILY MEMBER

FORM: ✒ AUTHENTIC FORM REQUIRED

FORM REQUIREMENTS: A **Waiver of Interment Rights** must be executed **in authentic form** before a **notary public and two competent witnesses**, as it constitutes a **relinquishment of a real right in immovable property**. Under **La. R.S. 8:812(B)**, the right of interment is treated as a heritable and transferable property right, and any act that abandons, donates, or waives that right must meet the formalities required for acts affecting immovables. The authentic form ensures the waiver is legally effective, properly recordable, and self-proving under **C.C. art. 1833**.

PURPOSE: Allows a person entitled to interment to relinquish that right in favor of another family member.

CITATION: La. R.S. 8:806 – Waiver or Assignment of Right of Interment
"The right of interment may be waived or assigned by a person having such right, provided the waiver or assignment is in writing and filed with the Cemetery Authority."

DESCRIPTION: Used to transfer burial priority within a family. Once filed, the waiver becomes part of the cemetery's permanent ownership records and authorizes burial of the substitute designee.

WAIVER OF INTERMENT RIGHTS
IN FAVOR OF ANOTHER FAMILY MEMBER

STATE OF LOUISIANA
PARISH OF ________________

BE IT KNOWN, that on this ____ day of ______________, 20____, before me, the undersigned Notary Public, duly commissioned and qualified in and for the Parish and State aforesaid, PERSONALLY CAME AND APPEARED:

____, domiciled in the Parish of
___________________________, State of Louisiana, herein "Appearer," who declared that:

The APPEARER is a lawful heir, successor, or family member of __________________________, who holds or held interment rights in the following described interment space located within ___________________ Cemetery:

Building/Location	**Section**	**Row/Unit**	**Space No(s).**

The APPEARER acknowledges that under **La. R.S. 8:803**, **8:804**, and **8:805**, the right of interment is a limited right or servitude, not a fee ownership interest, and that such right may be transferred or waived only in accordance with law and cemetery regulations.

The APPEARER hereby **waives, releases, and renounces** any and all interest, title, and right of interment or claim of interment in the above-described space, together with all related privileges, in favor of: ____, domiciled in the Parish of __________________, State of Louisiana, herein referred to as *"Beneficiary."*

This waiver is made voluntarily and with full knowledge of the APPEARER'S rights under Louisiana law and the regulations of the CEMETERY AUTHORITY.

BENEFICIARY hereby accepts this waiver and acknowledges the transfer of the APPEARER'S right of interment as set forth herein, subject to all applicable rules and regulations of the Cemetery and the provisions of *Title 8, Louisiana Revised Statutes.*

This Waiver of Interment Rights shall be filed in the records of the CEMETERY AUTHORITY pursuant to **La. R.S. 8:703** and **8:803(C)**,

This act shall be effective immediately upon execution and acceptance by the BENEFICIARY, acknowledgment before a Notary Public, and acceptance by the CEMETERY AUTHORITY.

THUS, DONE AND SIGNED in the Parish and State aforesaid, on the day, month, and year first above written, in the presence of the undersigned competent witnesses and Notary Public, after due reading of the whole.

WITNESSES:	**APPEARER:**
______________________________	______________________________
Signature of Witness	Signature of Appearer
______________________________	______________________________, APPEARER
Printed Name of Witness	Printed Name of Appearer
	BENEFICIARY:
______________________________	______________________________
Signature of Witness	Signature of Beneficiary
______________________________	______________________________, BENEFICIARY
Printed Name of Witness	Printed Name of Beneficiary

____
Signature of Notary

Printed Notary Name: ______________________________
Notary ID or Bar Roll No.: ______________
My Commission is for Life

PART III

INTERMENT AND DISINTERMENT

FORM 3.1

AUTHORIZATION FOR INTERMENT

FORM: 🚫 **NO NOTARIZATION REQUIRED**

FORM REQUIREMENTS: It authorizes burial or entombment and is signed by the person with the **right of disposition** under La. R.S. 8:655. The cemetery relies on the signature under private form; notarization is optional and only when additional proof of authority is desired.

PURPOSE: Provides written authorization by the person having legal control of disposition to permit the burial, entombment, or inurnment of human remains.

CITATION: La. R.S. 8:655 — Right of Disposition; Order of Priority
"The right to control interment of the remains of a deceased person, unless otherwise directed by the decedent, vests in the surviving spouse, or, in the absence thereof, the next of kin, in the order named by law."

DESCRIPTION: Used by cemetery authorities to confirm who has the lawful authority to order the interment. Includes name of decedent, interment location, and authorizing signature. Maintained permanently in the interment file.

AUTHORIZATION FOR INTERMENT

I, ____ (Name of Authorizing Party), being the ☐ spouse ☐ next of kin ☐ legal representative of the decedent named below, and whose mailing address is ____ do hereby authorize ____ Cemetery to inter the remains of:

Full Name of Deceased: ____

Date of Death: ______________________ **Place of Death:** ______________________

Age: ______ **Sex:** ______ **Religion (if applicable):** ______________________

in the space(s) designated in the books of ____________ Cemetery as:

Building/Location	**Section**	**Row/Unit**	**Space No(s).**

Funeral Home: ____

Funeral Director: ____

Funeral Home Phone: ____________________________

Service Date and Time: ____________________________

Special Instructions (if any): ____

I certify that I am the person legally entitled to authorize this interment under **La. R.S. 8:655**, and I hereby release and hold harmless ____________________ CEMETERY AUTHORITY, its employees, and representatives from any liability arising from the interment as authorized herein.

Executed this _____ day of ______________, 20______.

____
Signature of Authorizing Party

____
Printed Name of Authorizing Party

____
Relationship to Deceased

FORM 3.2

AGREEMENT FOR TEMPORARY INTERMENT

FORM: 🚫 **NO NOTARIZATION REQUIRED**

FORM REQUIREMENTS: It is a temporary administrative agreement between the family and the cemetery for provisional placement of remains. Private signature suffices; a notarial acknowledgment may be used for evidentiary value, but is not mandated.

PURPOSE: Authorizes temporary storage or entombment of human remains when permanent burial cannot immediately take place.

CITATION: **La. R.S. 8:659 – Disinterment and Reinterment; Authorization**
"No human remains shall be removed from a cemetery without the written authorization of the Cemetery Authority and the person having the right of interment."

DESCRIPTION: Used when conditions such as inclement weather, construction delays, or pending burial arrangements prevent immediate final interment. Specifies temporary location, reason, and intended date of final disposition.

AGREEMENT FOR TEMPORARY INTERMENT

This agreement is made between ____ herein "Promisor(s)" and __________________ Cemetery, herein "Cemetery" to inter the remains of ____________________________, herein "Decedent" within a temporary receiving vault as defined in **La. R.S. 8:1(43)** in _________________ Cemetery in the Parish of ________________________, State of Louisiana, for temporary burial purposes of human remains and no other.

CEMETERY grants to the PROMISOR above temporary interment in space(s) described in the books of ___________________ Cemetery as:

Building/Location	**Section**	**Row/Unit**	**Space No(s).**

herein, "Space A," until such a time that permanent burial is possible in crypt(s)/lot(s) described in the books of ___________________ Cemetery as:

Building/Location	**Section**	**Row/Unit**	**Space No(s).**

herein "Space B".

The PROMISOR hereby grants CEMETERY authorization to disinter from SPACE A and reinter the DECEDENT in SPACE B at its discretion without notice as soon as the CEMETERY deems such disinterment and reinterment safe, reasonable, and prudent. There shall be no charges for this temporary interment. This document shall also serve as a permanent interment order.

____
Signature of Promisor

____
Authorized Representative of Cemetery

____
Signature of Promisor

____
Date

FORM 3.3

AUTHORIZATION TO DISINTER OR REINTER HUMAN REMAINS

FORM: ✏ **NOTARIZATION REQUIRED**

FORM REQUIREMENTS: La. R.S. 8:659 requires written authorization by the person(s) with the right of disposition, and notarization authenticates the identity and consent of the authorizing party. The notary's acknowledgment ensures the cemetery can act without liability.

PURPOSE: Records the written consent of the lawful party to remove remains from one burial space and reinter them elsewhere.

CITATION: La. R.S. 8:659(A) – Disinterment and Reinterment; Authorization
"No human remains shall be removed from a cemetery without the written authorization of the Cemetery Authority and the person having the right of interment."

DESCRIPTION: Required before any disinterment. Lists decedent, current location, proposed new location, and authorizing individuals. Signed by the Cemetery Authority and filed permanently.

AUTHORIZATION ORDER
TO DISINTER/REINTER HUMAN REMAINS
WITHIN THE SAME CEMETERY

STATE OF LOUISIANA
PARISH OF ________________________

BEFORE ME, the undersigned Notary Public, commissioned and qualified in and for the Parish and State aforesaid, DID PERSONALLY APPEAR:

___________________, declaring him/herself to be of the full age of majority, herein "Grantor."

GRANTOR declares that he/she is the next of kin of _____________________ herein "Decedent," presently interred in ______________ Cemetery, herein "Cemetery." GRANTOR authorizes the CEMETERY to remove the remains of the DECEDENT who is currently interred in the following location:

Building/Location	**Section**	**Row/Unit**	**Space No(s).**

It is further agreed and understood that the remains are to be transferred and re-interred within ____________________ Cemetery in the following location:

Building/Location	**Section**	**Row/Unit**	**Space No(s).**

I, the undersigned, fully understand that it may be necessary to dispose of the casket and other material in connection with the above, and we do hereby authorize the cemetery to take whatever actions are necessary. We further agree to pay the cemetery a dis-interment and re-interment fee in the sum of __________________________ Dollars ($_________), for performing this service. Permission is hereby granted for the disinterment and reinterment. Costs for services are to be paid prior to any service being performed by me, the accredited undersigned.

I do hereby agree to indemnify and hold harmless ________________ Cemetery from and against all claims, suits, actions, proceedings (formal or informal), investigations, judgments, deficiencies, damages, settlements, liabilities and legal and other expenses (including legal fees and expenses of attorneys chosen by the CEMETERY as and when incurred arising out of or based upon any act or omissions or any alleged act or alleged omission by the Cemetery and/or Diocese in connection with any of the above.

GRANTOR:

____
Signature of Grantor

____
Printed Name of Grantor

SWORN TO AND SUBSCRIBED before me on
this ____ day of ______________, 20____

____
Signature of Notary

Printed Notary Name: ______________________________
Notary ID or Bar Roll No.: _______________
My Commission is for Life

FORM 3.4

CERTIFICATE OF INTERMENT COMPLETION

FORM: 🚫 **NO NOTARIZATION REQUIRED**

FORM REQUIREMENTS: It is an **internal cemetery application** used to request and record approval for disinterment or reinterment. The applicant and Cemetery Authority sign the document under private signature, and it remains in the cemetery's operational files. Notarization is optional if the cemetery wishes additional verification for outside submission to health or municipal authorities.

PURPOSE: Certifies that an interment has been completed in accordance with Louisiana law and cemetery procedures.

CITATION: La. R.S. 8:803(D) – Record of Interments
"Each Cemetery Authority shall maintain accurate records of every interment, including the name of the decedent, date of interment, and exact location."

DESCRIPTION: Executed by the cemetery sexton or manager immediately after burial. Confirms that interment was correctly performed and records all required details.

CERTIFICATE OF INTERMENT COMPLETION

Cemetery: ____

Building/Location	**Section**	**Row/Unit**	**Space No(s).**

This is to certify that the remains of __________________________________ (Name of Decedent) were interred/entombed/inurned in this cemetery on the _____ day of ______________, 20_____, in accordance with Louisiana law and cemetery regulations.

Funeral Home ____
Director ____
Burial Permit No. _________________________

____
Signature of Authorized Cemetery Representative

____
Printed Name of Authorized Cemetery Representative

____
Date

FORM 3.5

CERTIFICATION OF DISINTERMENT AND REINTERMENT BY SEXTON

FORM: 🚫 **NO NOTARIZATION REQUIRED**

FORM REQUIREMENTS: This form does **not require notarization.** It is a verification completed by the sexton or Cemetery Authority confirming that disinterment and reinterment were carried out in accordance with **La. R.S. 8:659(C)**. The form is signed under private signature by the authorized employee and filed in the cemetery's permanent operational records. A notary acknowledgment is optional but not legally required.

PURPOSE: Provides official confirmation by the cemetery sexton that disinterment and reinterment were completed under proper authority.

CITATION: La. R.S. 8:659(C) – Certificate of Disinterment and Reinterment
"A certificate of disinterment and reinterment shall be issued by the Cemetery Authority or sexton and kept as part of the cemetery's permanent records."

DESCRIPTION: Completed by the sexton or designated cemetery official. The report provides the date, method, and new location of the remains. Maintained in both the disinterment and reinterment files.

CERTIFICATION OF DISINTERMENT AND REINTERMENT BY CEMETERY SEXTON

ON THIS _____ day of ____________________, 20_____, I, the undersigned, hereby certify that I am the duly appointed Sexton of ____________________ Cemetery, located at ______________________ ___________________________in the Parish of ___________________________, State of Louisiana.

I further certify that I PERSONALLY SUPERVISED AND WITNESSED the disinterment and reinterment of the remains of:

_______________________________________ herein "Decedent,"

who was disinterred from a space designated in the books of ____________ Cemetery as:

Building/Location	**Section**	**Row/Unit**	**Space No(s).**

and reinterred in a space designated in the books of the same Cemetery as:

Building/Location	**Section**	**Row/Unit**	**Space No(s).**

This certification is made to document that the relocation of the above-named DECEDENT'S remains occurred on the date aforesaid and that said disinterment/reinterment was supervised by the Cemetery sexton in accordance with **LA R.S. 37:848**.

THUS DONE, SIGNED, AND ATTESTED:

____

Signature of Sexton

FOR _____________ CEMETERY, INC.

By _________________________________

Printed Name of Sexton

FORM 3.6

APPLICATION AND AUTHORIZATION FOR DISINTERMENT / REINTERMENT

FORM: 🚫 **NO NOTARIZATION REQUIRED**

FORM REQUIREMENTS: This form does **not require notarization.** It serves as the cemetery's internal application for initiating and approving disinterment or reinterment. Both the applicant and Cemetery Authority sign under private signature; the document is filed in operational records. A notarial acknowledgment may be added if the document is later submitted to the health department or court.

PURPOSE: Serves as the cemetery's formal application and approval form for disinterment and reinterment actions.

CITATION: La. R.S. 8:659(B) – Record of Disinterment and Reinterment
"When disinterment and reinterment are authorized, the Cemetery Authority shall keep a record of the date, location, and parties involved."

DESCRIPTION: Documents the requestor, authority granting approval, date, and disposition details. Becomes a required part of the cemetery's permanent record system.

APPLICATION AND AUTHORIZATION FOR DISINTERMENT / REINTERMENT

I, ____ (Applicant), being the ☐ next of kin ☐ legal representative of the decedent named below, hereby apply for permission to disinter the remains of:

Name of Deceased: ____

Date of Death: _____________________________

Presently Interred in the space(s) designated in the books of __________ Cemetery as:

Building/Location	**Section**	**Row/Unit**	**Space No(s).**

Purpose of Disinterment: ☐ Reinterment in the same cemetery ☐ Transfer to another cemetery ☐ Cremation after removal ☐ Other: _____________________________

Requested Reinterment location, if within the same Cemetery:

Building/Location	**Section**	**Row/Unit**	**Space No(s).**

Requested Date: _____________________________

Applicant acknowledges that all removals and reinterments will comply with **La. R.S. 8:659**, local health regulations, and any court or Board orders if applicable.

Executed this _____ day of ______________, 20_____.

Applicant's Signature: ____

Printed Name: ____

Relationship to Deceased: ____

Address: ____

FORM 3.7

CHAIN OF CUSTODY RECORD FOR DISINTERMENT

FORM: 🚫 **NO NOTARIZATION REQUIRED**

FORM REQUIREMENTS: This form does **not require notarization.** It is an internal tracking record documenting each custody handoff of remains during disinterment. Each handler signs under private signature. It functions as a compliance log, not a legal instrument.

PURPOSE: Establishes a verifiable chain of custody during disinterment and reinterment of human remains.

CITATION: **La. Admin. Code tit. 46, Pt. XIII, §1103 – Records of Disinterment**
"Cemetery authorities shall maintain permanent records of each disinterment and reinterment, identifying the date, parties present, and final resting place."

DESCRIPTION: Used by cemetery personnel and funeral directors to document each transfer of custody. Ensures compliance with regulatory and public health standards.

CHAIN OF CUSTODY RECORD
DISINTERMENT TO ANOTHER CEMETERY

Deceased: ____

Date of Death: ____________________________

Original Burial Location in ____________________ Cemetery:

Building/Location	**Section**	**Row/Unit**	**Space No(s).**

Date and Time of Disinterment: ____________________________ at _________AM / PM

Authorized by: (attach Application or Court Order) ____________________________

Funeral Home / Director Supervising Removal:
Name: ____ License No.: __________

Funeral Home: ____

Phone: ____________________________

Transported To: ____ Cemetery

All parties involved certify that the remains of the above-named individual were handled with dignity and in accordance with **La. R.S. 8:659** and all health and safety regulations.

Cemetery Authority Representative: ____

Title: ____________________________________ **Date:** ______________________

FORM 3.8

NOTICE OF PROPOSED DISINTERMENT (PUBLIC OR FAMILY NOTICE)

FORM: 🛇 **NO NOTARIZATION REQUIRED**

FORM REQUIREMENTS: This form does **not require notarization.** It is executed under private signature by the Cemetery Authority to meet the notice requirement of **La. R.S. 8:660(A)**. Notarization is unnecessary unless the cemetery later files an affidavit of posting or publication, which is why the notarization section is provided.

PURPOSE: Provides notice to heirs or the public when consent for disinterment cannot be obtained.

CITATION: La. R.S. 8:660(A) – Notice of Intent to Disinter
"When the consent of the person vested with control cannot be obtained, notice of intent to disinter shall be given to all known heirs and published as required by law."

DESCRIPTION: Used by the cemetery to document that required notices were mailed and/or published before proceeding, and filed with proof of publication and mailing affidavits.

NOTICE OF PROPOSED DISINTERMENT

Date: ____________________________

Notice is hereby given that _____________________ Cemetery, located at ____, in the Parish of _______________________, Louisiana, has received a request to disinter the remains of:

Name of Deceased: ____
Date of Death: ____________________________
Current Burial Location:

Building/Location	**Section**	**Row/Unit**	**Space No(s).**

The purpose of the disinterment is ☐ reinterment within the same cemetery ☐ transfer to another cemetery ☐ cremation following removal ☐ other: ____________________________

Any person having a legal objection or superior right of control to the remains must submit a written notice to the Cemetery Authority within thirty (30) days of the date of this notice.

Authorized Representative: ____
Title: ____________________________________
Signature: _______________________________

FOR PUBLIC NOTICE (optional):

This notice shall be published one time in the official journal of the Parish of _____________________, and a copy shall be posted at the cemetery entrance for at least ten (10) days prior to disinterment.

Date Posted: _______________________ Posted By: ____________________________

NOTARIAL AFFIDAVIT OF POSTING / PUBLICATION

(optional)

State of Louisiana
Parish of ______________________________

BEFORE ME, the undersigned Notary Public, personally appeared ________________________________, who, after being duly sworn, stated that the foregoing Notice of Proposed Disinterment was posted and/or published as required above.

SWORN TO AND SUBSCRIBED before me on
this ____ day of ______________, 20____

____
Signature of Notary

Printed Notary Name: ______________________________
Notary ID or Bar Roll No.: ______________
My Commission is for Life

FORM 3.9

CERTIFICATE OF REINTERMENT

FORM: 🚫 **NO NOTARIZATION REQUIRED**

FORM REQUIREMENTS: This form does **not require notarization.** It is completed by the sexton or Cemetery Authority to certify that reinterment has been accomplished in accordance with law and is filed in the cemetery's permanent records.

PURPOSE: Serves as documentary proof of lawful reinterment after remains have been relocated.

CITATION: **La. R.S. 8:659(D) – Record of Reinterment**
"Upon completion of reinterment, the Cemetery Authority shall enter into its records the date and new location of the remains."

DESCRIPTION: Created after reinterment to confirm final disposition. The system provides new section, lot, and space numbers and replaces prior burial record entries.

CERTIFICATE OF REINTERMENT

Deceased: ______________________________

Date of Original Interment: ______________________

Date of Disinterment: ______________________

Original Burial Location:

Building/Location	**Section**	**Row/Unit**	**Space No(s).**

New Reinterment Location:

Building/Location	**Section**	**Row/Unit**	**Space No(s).**

☐ Same Cemetery ☐ Transferred To: ______________________ Cemetery

This certifies that the remains of the above-named individual were lawfully disinterred and reinterred in accordance with **La. R.S. 8:659**, and that all necessary authorizations were obtained prior to the disinterment.

Date of Reinterment: ______________________

Funeral Director (if applicable): ______________________________

____
Signature of Cemetery Representative

____
Printed Name of Cemetery Representative

____
Title of Cemetery Representative

____
Date

FORM 3.10

CREMATED REMAINS RELEASE FORM

FORM: 🚫 **NO NOTARIZATION REQUIRED**

FORM REQUIREMENTS: This document is valid as a written certification under **La. R.S. 8:812(A)**. No notarization or witnesses are required for conveyances or transfers executed by the **Cemetery. A notarial acknowledgment, al**though not required, is preferable.

PURPOSE: Authorizes the release of cremated remains to the legally entitled individual or representative.

CITATION: La. R.S. 37:876(A)(2) – Release of Cremated Remains
"Cremated remains shall be released only to the person authorized to control disposition or to a person designated in writing by that individual."

DESCRIPTION: Ensures cremated remains are released to the correct party. Includes identification verification and date of release. Signed by both the releasing employee and the recipient.

CREMATED REMAINS RELEASE FORM

Cemetery / Facility Name: ______________________________
Address: ______________________________
Phone: ____________________

Name of Deceased: ______________________________
Date of Death: ____________________
Date of Cremation: ____________________
Crematory Name: ______________________________

The undersigned hereby acknowledges receipt of the cremated remains of the above-named individual from ______________ Cemetery and certifies that they are legally entitled to receive and control said remains under **La. R.S. 8:655**.

Recipient (Name): ______________________________
Relationship to Deceased: ____________________
Address: ______________________________
Phone: ____________________
Date of Release: ____________________

Recipient Signature: ______________________________

Cemetery Representative: ______________________________

NOTARIAL ACKNOWLEDGMENT (optional)

STATE OF LOUISIANA
PARISH OF ____________________

On this _____ day of ______________, 20_____, before me, the undersigned Notary Public, personally appeared ______________________________, who acknowledged receiving the cremated remains identified above.

____
Signature of Notary

Printed Notary Name: ______________________
Notary ID or Bar Roll No.: ______________
My Commission is for Life

FORM 3.11

CEMETERY WORK PERMIT / WORK ORDER FOR CONTRACTORS

FORM: 🚫 **NO NOTARIZATION REQUIRED**

FORM REQUIREMENTS: This form does **not require notarization.** It is an administrative authorization allowing monument or vault work on cemetery grounds. The cemetery and contractor execute the document under private signature.

PURPOSE: Grants written authorization for monument installation, repairs, or other construction within the cemetery.

CITATION: La. R.S. 8:308 — Rules and Regulations of Cemetery Authorities
"Each Cemetery Authority may make, adopt, amend, add to, revise, or abolish rules and regulations for the use, care, control, management, restriction, and protection of all or any part of its cemetery and for the other purposes specified in this Title."

DESCRIPTION: Required before any external contractor performs work. Ensures that all activity complies with cemetery safety, insurance, and appearance standards.

_________________ CEMETERY

____

____

OFFICIAL CEMETERY WORK PERMIT & CONTRACTOR AUTHORIZATION

PROJECT IDENTIFICATION

Date Issued	
Permit No.	
Issued by:	
Deceased:	
Owner / Family Representative:	
Phone / Email	

CEMETERY SPACE INFORMATION

Building/Location	**Section**	**Row/Unit**	**Space No(s).**

TYPE OF WORK (Check All That Apply)

- ☐ Grave Opening
- ☐ Grave Closing / Interment
- ☐ Disinterment / Reinterment
- ☐ Install Monument / Headstone
- ☐ Install or Remove Vault / Crypt Cover
- ☐ Foundation Installation
- ☐ Cleaning or Restoration Work
- ☐ Landscaping or Tree Removal
- ☐ Irrigation or Utility Work
- ☐ Mausoleum or Niche Work
- ☐ Other (describe):

____

CONTRACTOR INFORMATION

Company Name: ______________________________

Contact Person: ______________________________

Address: ______________________________

____

Phone: ______________________

Email: ______________________

Insurance Certificate No.: ____________________

Expiration: ______________

SCHEDULE OF WORK

Date(s) of Work: ____

Time(s): From ___________ a.m./p.m. To ___________ a.m./p.m.

Equipment to be Used: ______________________________________

Expected Duration: ____

All work shall be performed **only during approved hours** and **under the supervision of the Cemetery Authority** or its designee. Heavy equipment or vehicles must remain on approved access routes.

FEES AND CHARGES

Service Fees (check all that apply):		
☐ Grave Opening	$__________	**Total Fees Due:** $____________________
☐ Grave Closing	$__________	
☐ Disinterment / Reinterment	$__________	
☐ Monument / Marker Installation	$__________	**Payment Method:** ☐ Cash ☐ Check ☐ Credit ☐ Other: ____________
☐ Foundation / Concrete Work	$__________	
☐ Vault Handling or Placemen	$__________	**Receipt No.:** ____________________
☐ Permit Administration	$__________	**Date Paid:** ____________________
☐ Other (describe): ____________________________	$__________	

TERMS AND CONDITIONS

1. Contractors shall comply with all cemetery regulations and Louisiana laws governing cemetery operations.
2. Work must be conducted respectfully and safely; disruptive behavior or damage may result in the revocation of this permit.
3. Proof of current liability insurance must be on file before work begins.
4. The Cemetery reserves the right to inspect, suspend, or deny work at any time for cause.
5. Any damage to adjacent graves, markers, or landscaping must be repaired to the satisfaction of the Cemetery Authority.
6. All debris and materials must be removed from site immediately upon completion of work.
7. No work may commence until **fees are paid in full** and the permit is signed by both the Cemetery and Contractor.

Issued By (Cemetery Representative):	**Contractor Acknowledgment:**
	I have read and agree to comply with all conditions stated herein.
Name: ______________________________	Company: ______________________________
Title: ______________________________	Authorized Representative: __________________
Signature: ___________________________	Signature: ______________________________
Date: ______________________________	Date: __________________________________

NOTICE

This permit must be **kept on site** during all work. Unauthorized or unpermitted work is prohibited. Failure to comply may result in suspension of contractor privileges and revocation of future access.

PART IV

PERPETUAL CARE AND TRUST FUNDS

FORM 4.1

PERPETUAL CARE AGREEMENT

FORM: 🚫 **NO NOTARIZATION REQUIRED**

FORM REQUIREMENTS: This is a private contract between the purchaser and the Cemetery Authority setting forth the terms of perpetual care and trust fund contribution as required under **La. R.S. 8:454.** Execution under private signature of both parties is sufficient. If the agreement is attached to a recorded instrument or trust filing, a notarial acknowledgment should be added for evidentiary purposes.

PURPOSE: Establishes the purchaser's and Cemetery Authority's mutual obligations regarding the ongoing maintenance and preservation of the cemetery property under perpetual care.

CITATION: La. R.S. 8:454 — Establishment and Maintenance of Trust Fund
"Every Cemetery Authority operating a perpetual care cemetery shall establish and maintain a trust fund for the permanent maintenance and care of the cemetery and shall deposit into such fund not less than ten percent of the gross sales price of all interment spaces sold."

DESCRIPTION: Used to inform purchasers of the cemetery's perpetual care status, the percentage of proceeds dedicated to the fund, and the scope of maintenance covered. Ensures transparency and compliance with Title 8 funding requirements.

PERPETUAL CARE AGREEMENT

This Agreement, made this _____ day of __________________, 20_____, by and between

____________________ Cemetery, herein "Cemetery," and

____, herein "Purchaser."

Deposit to Perpetual Care Fund

A sum of $ ____________________ representing ___ % of the total sale price shall be deposited into the Perpetual Care Fund pursuant to **La. R.S. 8:454** in connection with purchaser of interment rights in the following burial location, designated in the books of ____________________ Cemetery as:

Building/Location	**Section**	**Row/Unit**	**Space No(s).**

Purpose of Fund
Income only from the fund shall be used for the general care, maintenance, and embellishment of the cemetery grounds, structures, and improvements.

Trust Administration
Funds are held in trust by ____ (Bank or Trust Company) under a written trust agreement on file with the Cemetery Authority.

Irrevocability
Deposits to the Perpetual Care Fund are permanent and shall not be withdrawn except as permitted by **La. R.S. 8:458 – 468**.

Executed this _______ day of ___________________, 20_____.

PURCHASER:

____
Signature of Purchaser

____
Printed Name of Purchaser

CEMETERY REPRESENTATIVE:

____
Signature of Cemetery Representative

____
Printed Name of Cemetery Representative

FORM 4.2

MONTHLY PERPETUAL CARE FUND WORKSHEET

FORM: 🚫 **NO NOTARIZATION REQUIRED**

FORM REQUIREMENTS: This is an internal financial record maintained by the Cemetery Authority to document deposits, income, and distributions related to the perpetual care trust. Signatures of authorized officers under private signature are sufficient; no witnesses or notary required.

PURPOSE: Records monthly deposits, withdrawals, income, and balances in the cemetery's perpetual care trust fund.

CITATION: **La. Admin. Code tit. 46, Pt. XIII, §1301 – Trust Fund Reporting Requirements**
"Every Cemetery Authority shall maintain accurate records of all perpetual care trust fund deposits, disbursements, and income, and shall file reports with the Louisiana Cemetery Board as required."

DESCRIPTION: Used by cemetery management to prepare monthly summaries of all trust fund activity. Serves as the basis for quarterly and annual filings with the Louisiana Cemetery Board.

MONTHLY PERPETUAL CARE FUND WORKSHEET

____________________ Cemetery

____

____

REPORT INFORMATION

Month of ____________________, 20_____

Date Prepared: ____________________________

Prepared By: ____

Title: ____

SUMMARY OF SALES AND REQUIRED DEPOSITS

Type of Transaction	Number of Contracts	Gross Sales / Receipts ($)	Deposit %	Amount Due to Trust ($)
Ground Spaces				
Mausoleum / Niche Spaces				
Perpetual Care Contracts (Sold Independently)				
Donated Spaces (Fair Value Basis)				
Other — Specify ________________________________				
TOTALS FOR MONTH				

DEPOSIT DETAILS

Date Deposited to Trustee/Bank: __________________________

Bank or Trustee Institution: ____

Account Name/Number: ____

Check or EFT No.: ____________________ Deposit Amount: $________________

Deposit Confirmed By: _________________________ Date Confirmed: _________________

FUND BALANCE AND ACTIVITY SUMMARY

Opening Balance (as of 1st of Month): $________________

Deposits This Month: $________________

Interest Earned / Income Credited: $________________

Withdrawals (if any): $________________

Closing Balance (as of End of Month): $________________

CERTIFICATION OF COMPLIANCE

I hereby certify that the foregoing information accurately represents all sales and perpetual care deposits for the month stated, and that funds have been deposited in accordance with La. R.S. 8:903 and all applicable regulations of the Louisiana Cemetery Board.

CEMETERY AUTHORITY REPRESENTATIVE:

Printed Name: ______________________________________

Title: ______________________________________

Signature: ______________________________________

Date: ______________________________________

TRUSTEE / BANK ACKNOWLEDGMENT (Optional)

Received By: ______________________________________

Institution: ______________________________________

Date of Receipt: ______________________________________

Verified Deposit Amount: $______________________________

Signature: ______________________________________

FORM 4.3

INVESTMENT / DISTRIBUTION AUTHORIZATION

FORM: 🚫 **NO NOTARIZATION REQUIRED**

FORM REQUIREMENTS: It is executed between the Cemetery Authority and the trustee or financial institution authorizing investment or disbursement of trust funds in accordance with **La. R.S. 8:458.** Both parties sign under private signature, as the agreement functions as an administrative authorization rather than a legal conveyance.

PURPOSE: Authorizes the trustee to invest or reinvest funds and to distribute income for cemetery maintenance in accordance with the trust agreement.

CITATION: La. R.S. 8:458 – Investment Authority of Trustee
"The trustee of every perpetual care trust fund shall have the power to invest and reinvest the principal in securities and obligations authorized by the trust instrument and approved by the Cemetery Authority, and income shall be used exclusively for cemetery care."

DESCRIPTION: Executed by the Cemetery Authority's board and trustee to confirm investment or distribution transactions and maintained as part of the cemetery's perpetual care compliance records.

INVESTMENT / DISTRIBUTION AUTHORIZATION

To: ___________________________________ (Trustee Institution)

Date: ____________________

Pursuant to our Perpetual Care Fund Trust Agreement, you are hereby authorized to:

☐ Invest $ ___________________ in ____

☐ Distribute income in the amount of $ ___________________ for cemetery maintenance expenses for the period ending ____________________.

Authorized Representative: ____

Title: _________________________________

Signature: ____________________________

Date: _________________________

Trustee Receipt Acknowledgment
Received and executed this _____ day of ______________, 20_____.
Authorized Trustee Officer: ____
Title: _________________________________
Signature: ____________________________

FORM 4.4

TRUSTEE ACKNOWLEDGMENT OF DEPOSIT

FORM: 🚫 **NO NOTARIZATION REQUIRED**

FORM REQUIREMENTS: It serves as written acknowledgment by the trustee of receipt of deposited funds as required under **La. R.S. 8:462.** The trustee's signature under private form suffices; notarization is optional if the cemetery requests a verified acknowledgment for audit or reporting.

PURPOSE: Provides the trustee's confirmation of receipt of trust fund deposits from the Cemetery Authority.

CITATION: La. R.S. 8:462 – Trustee Reporting and Acknowledgment
"The trustee of the perpetual care trust fund shall furnish to the Cemetery Authority and the board an annual statement of receipts, disbursements, and balance, and shall acknowledge receipt of each deposit."

DESCRIPTION: Used to document each trust deposit made. The signed acknowledgment serves as evidence of compliance with deposit requirements and is retained for audit by the Louisiana Cemetery Board.

TRUSTEE ACKNOWLEDGMENT OF DEPOSIT

Date: ___________________________

We hereby acknowledge receipt from _____________________________________ Cemetery Authority of the sum of $ ___________________, to be held in trust under the Perpetual Care Fund Agreement dated _______________________________, in accordance with **La. R.S. 8:458**.

Trustee Institution: ____

Authorized Officer: ____

Title: ___________________________________

Signature: ______________________________

Date: ______________________________

PART V

ABANDONED SPACES AND REMOVAL OF DEDICATION

FORM 5.1

NOTICE OF ABANDONED CEMETERY SPACE (POSTED NOTICE)

FORM: 🚫 **NO NOTARIZATION REQUIRED**

FORM REQUIREMENTS: This is an administrative notice posted at the main entrance of the cemetery pursuant to **La. R.S. 8:308.1(A)**. The Cemetery Authority signs it under private signature. Notarization is unnecessary unless an affidavit of posting will be recorded later. An optional Affidavit of posting is provided.

PURPOSE: Provides an official posted notice that a cemetery space appears to be abandoned, initiating the statutory process for reclaiming interment rights.

CITATION: La. R.S. 8:308.1 – Abandonment of Interment Spaces; Notice Requirements
"When the Cemetery Authority determines that an interment space appears to be abandoned, notice shall be posted at the main entrance of the cemetery and mailed to the last known address of the owner, if known."

DESCRIPTION: Used by cemetery management to begin formal proceedings for the reclamation of abandoned property. Posted for the required statutory period and kept with the cemetery's records as evidence of compliance.

PUBLIC NOTICE OF ABANDONED CEMETERY SPACE

Pursuant to **La. R.S. 8:905(B)**, notice is hereby given that interment rights to the following space in

______________________ Cemetery is presumed abandoned:

Building/Location	**Section**	**Row/Unit**	**Space No(s).**

If the owner or lawful heirs wish to assert their rights, they must contact the cemetery office at

____

(address/phone) within __________ (_____) days of this posting and publication.

Failure to respond will constitute a waiver of rights and authorize the Cemetery Authority to reclaim the space for future use as provided by law.

Dated this _____ day of ______________, 20_____.

Authorized Representative: ____
Title: __________________________________

AFFIDAVIT OF POSTING

(optional)

STATE OF LOUISIANA
PARISH OF ________________________

BEFORE ME, the undersigned Notary Public, PERSONALLY CAME AND APPEARED:

___________________________________,

who, after being duly sworn, stated that this notice was posted at the cemetery entrance and on the affected space on the date shown above.

SWORN TO AND SUBSCRIBED before me on
this ____ day of ______________, 20____

____
Signature of Notary

Printed Notary Name: ______________________________
Notary ID or Bar Roll No.: _______________
My Commission is for Life

FORM 5.2

NOTICE OF ABANDONMENT (NEWSPAPER PUBLICATION)

FORM: 🛇 **NO NOTARIZATION REQUIRED**

FORM REQUIREMENTS: It is prepared for publication in a newspaper of general circulation in the parish as required by **La. R.S. 8:308.1(B)**. The publisher's affidavit of publication—executed separately—will be notarized by the newspaper, but the cemetery's notice itself need not be. Optional Affidavit of Publication provided.

PURPOSE: Provides public notice through publication in a local newspaper that a space is considered abandoned under Louisiana law.

CITATION: La. R.S. 8:308.1(B) – Publication of Notice
"The Cemetery Authority shall publish notice of the abandoned interment space once a week for two consecutive weeks in a newspaper of general circulation in the parish where the cemetery is located."

DESCRIPTION: Used concurrently with posted notice to complete statutory notification. A copy of the published notice and affidavit of publication is attached to the cemetery's file.

PUBLIC NOTICE OF ABANDONED CEMETERY SPACE

Pursuant to **La. R.S. 8:905(B)**, notice is hereby given that interment rights to the following space in ____ Cemetery are presumed abandoned:

Building/Location	**Section**	**Row/Unit**	**Space No(s).**

If the owner or lawful heirs wish to assert their rights, they must contact the cemetery office at ____ (address/phone) within __________ (_____) days of this publication.

Failure to respond will constitute a waiver of rights and authorize the Cemetery Authority to reclaim the space for future use as provided by law.

Dated this _____ day of ______________, 20_____.

Authorized Representative: ____

Title: __________________________________

AFFIDAVIT OF PUBLICATION

(Optional)

STATE OF LOUISIANA
PARISH OF ___________________________

BEFORE ME, the undersigned Notary Public, PERSONALLY CAME AND APPEARED:

______________________________________,

who, after being duly sworn, stated that this notice was published in ________________________ and on the date shown above.

SWORN TO AND SUBSCRIBED before me on this ____ day of ______________, 20____

____
Signature of Notary

Printed Notary Name: ________________________________
Notary ID or Bar Roll No.: _______________
My Commission is for Life

FORM 5.3

CERTIFICATE / AFFIDAVIT OF POSTING AND PUBLICATION

FORM: ✏️ **NOTARIZATION REQUIRED**

FORM REQUIREMENTS: This form **must be notarized.** It constitutes an affidavit confirming compliance with the posting and publication requirements of **La. R.S. 8:308.1(C)**. The affiant (usually the cemetery manager) swears under oath before a notary that the required notices were properly given.

PURPOSE: Certifies that required notices of abandonment were posted and published according to law.

CITATION: La. R.S. 8:308.1(C) – Proof of Notice
"Proof of notice by affidavit of the person posting or publishing such notice shall be filed in the records of the Cemetery Authority and maintained permanently."

DESCRIPTION: Executed by the cemetery manager or designee to certify completion of notice requirements. Serves as evidentiary proof before any formal declaration of abandonment.

AFFIDAVIT OF NOTICE POSTING AND PUBLICATION

STATE OF LOUISIANA
PARISH OF ___________________________

BEFORE ME, the undersigned Notary Public, PERSONALLY APPEARED:

____, a person of the age of majority, who declares that he/she is the duly authorized representative of the Cemetery Authority having jurisdiction over the property described below herein "Affiant",

WHO DECLARED THAT:

In compliance with **La. R.S. 8:905**, the Cemetery Authority has posted and published notice of its intent to declare interment rights in the following space abandoned:

Building/Location	**Section**	**Row/Unit**	**Space No(s).**

Posted at Cemetery Entrance on ___________________ Published in ___________________ (Newspaper) on ___________________.

Executed this _____ day of ______________, 20_____.

____
Signature of Affiant

____
Printed Name of Affiant

____
Title of Affiant

SWORN TO AND SUBSCRIBED before me on this ____ day of ______________, 20____

____
Signature of Notary

Printed Notary Name: ________________________________
Notary ID or Bar Roll No.: ________________
My Commission is for Life

FORM 5.4

AFFIDAVIT OF NO RESPONSE AFTER NOTICE

FORM: ✎ **NOTARIZATION REQUIRED**

FORM REQUIREMENTS: It is a sworn statement by the Cemetery Authority that no claimant responded within the statutory period following notice under **La. R.S. 8:308.2(A)**. The affidavit is executed before a Louisiana notary using a jurat form.

PURPOSE: Declares that no response or claim was received from the owner or heirs after expiration of the posted and published notice period.

CITATION: La. R.S. 8:308.2 – Reversion of Abandoned Interment Spaces
"If no person entitled to the interment rights responds within the period stated in the notice, the Cemetery Authority may declare the space abandoned and may resell or reassign the rights in accordance with this Title."

DESCRIPTION: Prepared following the statutory waiting period. Confirms that all efforts at contact were made and that no claimant came forward. Filed with the permanent record to justify the reversion of rights.

AFFIDAVIT OF NO RESPONSE AFTER NOTICE

STATE OF LOUISIANA
PARISH OF ___________________________

BEFORE ME, the undersigned Notary Public, PERSONALLY APPEARED:

___________________________, a person of the age of majority and a domiciliary of
_________________________ Parish, Louisiana,

who, after being duly sworn, stated:

1. That the Cemetery Authority posted and published notice of abandonment on the dates shown in the Certificate of Notice Posting and Publication.
2. That no claim, objection, or response was received within ninety (90) days therein.
3. That the space identified as:

Building/Location	**Section**	**Row/Unit**	**Space No(s).**

is presumed abandoned.

Executed this _____ day of ______________, 20_____.

____
Signature of Affiant

____
Printed Name of Affiant

____
Title of Affiant

SWORN TO AND SUBSCRIBED before me on
this ____ day of ______________, 20____

____
Signature of Notary

Printed Notary Name: ______________________________
Notary ID or Bar Roll No.: ________________
My Commission is for Life

FORM *5.5*

BOARD RESOLUTION DECLARING SPACE ABANDONED

FORM: 🚫 **NO NOTARIZATION REQUIRED**

FORM REQUIREMENTS: This form does **not require notarization.** It is an internal governing resolution adopted by the cemetery's board pursuant to **La. R.S. 8:308.2(B)**. Board officers sign it under private signature. If the resolution is to be filed or recorded, a notarial acknowledgment may be added.

PURPOSE: Provides formal board action declaring specific cemetery space(s) legally abandoned and reverting to the cemetery's control.

CITATION: La. R.S. 8:308.2(B) – Declaration of Abandonment
"The governing authority of the cemetery may, by resolution, declare such space abandoned upon completion of all notice requirements."

DESCRIPTION: Signed and dated by members of the cemetery's governing board. Becomes the official internal action confirming abandonment before the space is returned to the market or reassigned.

RESOLUTION DECLARING ABANDONMENT OF CEMETERY SPACE

At a meeting of the Board of Directors / Trustees of ________________________________
Cemetery Authority, held on the _____ day of ______________, 20_____, the following resolution was adopted:

BE IT RESOLVED, that having complied with the notice requirements of **La. R.S. 8:905**, and having received no response from any owner or heir, the Board hereby declares the interment rights in:

Building/Location	**Section**	**Row/Unit**	**Space No(s).**

to be **abandoned** and returns said space to the CEMETERY AUTHORITY for future use.

Adopted by majority vote this _____ day of ______________, 20_____.

Chairperson: ____________________________________

Secretary: ____________________________________

(Seal if applicable)

NOTARIAL ACKNOWLEDGMENT (optional)

STATE OF LOUISIANA
PARISH OF ______________________

SUBSCRIBED AND ACKNOWLEDGED before me this _______day of __________________, 20_____.

____
Signature of Notary

Printed Notary Name: ___________________________
Notary ID or Bar Roll No.: _______________
My Commission is for Life

FORM 5.6

APPLICATION FOR REMOVAL OF DEDICATION

FORM: 🚫 **NO NOTARIZATION REQUIRED**

FORM REQUIREMENTS: This form does **not require notarization.** It is the written application submitted to the Louisiana Cemetery Board under **La. R.S. 8:305.1(A)** requesting removal of dedication from unused property. The application is executed under private signature by the Cemetery Authority.

PURPOSE: Used by a Cemetery Authority to request that the Louisiana Cemetery Board approve the removal of cemetery dedication from unused land.

CITATION: La. R.S. 8:305.1 – Removal of Dedication
"Any Cemetery Authority seeking to remove the dedication of cemetery property shall apply in writing to the Louisiana Cemetery Board, setting forth the reasons and the proposed use of the property."

DESCRIPTION: Initiates the process for removing dedication on land no longer needed for interments. Submitted with supporting documentation, including maps, board resolutions, and evidence of notice to lot owners.

APPLICATION FOR REMOVAL OF DEDICATION

To the Honorable ______________________________,

Judge of ________________ Court / Louisiana Cemetery Board:

The undersigned Cemetery Authority petitions for approval to remove the dedication from the following parcel of cemetery land, being no longer used for burial purposes:

Legal DESCRIPTION: ____

Area (Acres / Sq Ft): __________________

The Authority certifies that (1) no burials exist in the portion to be removed, (2) all notices have been given as required by law, and (3) approval of this application will not affect any occupied lots.

Executed this _____ day of ______________, 20_____.

____

Signature of Authorized Representative

____

Printed Name of Authorized Representative

____

Title of Cemetery Representative

FORM 5.7

AFFIDAVIT OF REMOVAL OF DEDICATION

FORM: **AUTHENTIC FORM REQUIRED**

FORM REQUIREMENTS: This form **must be notarized in Authentic Form** under **La. R.S. 8:305.1(C)**, once removal of dedication is approved, the Cemetery Authority must execute and record a notarized affidavit in the parish conveyance records confirming completion of the process.

PURPOSE: Certifies completion of the process of removing dedication from cemetery land as authorized by the Louisiana Cemetery Board.

CITATION: La. R.S. 8:305.1(C) – Recordation of Removal
"When the board approves the removal of dedication, the Cemetery Authority shall execute and record an affidavit of removal in the conveyance records of the parish in which the cemetery is situated."

DESCRIPTION: Executed by the Cemetery Authority after receiving state approval and recorded in parish conveyance records to officially terminate cemetery status for the designated property.

AFFIDAVIT OF REMOVAL OF DEDICATION

STATE OF LOUISIANA
PARISH OF ________________________

BE IT KNOWN that on this _____ day of ______________, 20_____ BEFORE ME, the undersigned Notary Public, duly commissioned and qualified in and for the Parish and State aforesaid, and in the presence of the undersigned competent witnesses, personally came and appeared:

____, a person of the age of majority, whose permanent mailing address is ____, and who is domiciled in ________________ Parish, Louisiana, and who declares that he/she is the duly authorized representative of the Cemetery Authority having jurisdiction over the property described below herein "Appearer",

WHO DECLARED THAT:

1. Pursuant to judgment of the ________________ Court/authorization by the Louisiana Cemetery Board, the **dedication of the following property for cemetery purposes has been lawfully removed**:

Legal Description:

____

____

____

____

(Attach full legal DESCRIPTION of property or reference to recorded plat or survey.)

2. No **human remains exist within the described property**, and the land has been **discontinued for cemetery purposes**.
3. This act is executed for **recordation in the conveyance records** of ____________________ Parish, Louisiana, in accordance with **La. R.S. 8:312**, to provide public notice that the cemetery dedication has been formally removed and the property has been restored to ordinary use.

THUS DONE AND SIGNED at ______________________, Louisiana, on the day, month, and year first above written, in the presence of the undersigned competent witnesses and me, Notary Public, after due reading of the whole.

WITNESSES:	**APPEARER:**
______________________________	______________________________
Signature of Witness	Signature of Appearer
______________________________	______________________________
Printed Name of Witness	Printed Name of Appearer
______________________________	
Signature of Witness	
______________________________	
Printed Name of Witness	

____
Signature of Notary

Printed Notary Name: ______________________________
Notary ID or Bar Roll No.: ______________
My Commission is for Life

PART VI

MISCELLANEOUS

FORM 6.1

SWORN STATEMENT OF FACTS

FORM: ✏ **NOTARIZATION REQUIRED**

FORM REQUIREMENTS: This is an affidavit made under oath before a Louisiana notary. The affiant swears to the truth of the facts contained in the document, and the notary completes a **jurat** confirming personal appearance, identity, and oath. This form is often used to support cemetery or family claims requiring verified statements.

PURPOSE: Provides a general affidavit for use by the Cemetery Authority or individuals when facts must be attested under oath.

CITATION: La. R.S. 35:2 – Notarial Acts
"Notaries public are authorized to receive acknowledgments, administer oaths, and make affidavits of any acts or matters authorized by law."

DESCRIPTION: Used to formally declare factual information related to cemetery operations, ownership, or transactions. May be attached as supporting documentation to other filings.

SWORN STATEMENT OF FACTS

STATE OF LOUISIANA
PARISH OF ____________________________

BEFORE ME, the undersigned Notary Public, PERSONALLY CAME AND APPEARED:

____

a person of full age of majority, domiciled in ____________________ Parish, Louisiana, whose Date of Birth is___________________, hereby attest:

1. ____
2. ____
3. ____
4. ____
5. ____
6. ____
7. ____
8. ____

AFFIANT certifies that these statements are true and correct to the best of their knowledge and belief.

AFFIANT:

____
Signature of Affiant

____
Printed Name of Affiant

____
Date

SWORN TO AND SUBSCRIBED before me on
this ____ day of ______________, 20____

____
Signature of Notary

Printed Notary Name: ______________________________
Notary ID or Bar Roll No.: _______________
My Commission is for Life

FORM 6.2

WITNESS STATEMENT FORM

FORM: ✏ **NOTARIZATION REQUIRED**

FORM REQUIREMENTS: It is a sworn declaration by a witness regarding relevant facts or observations relating to a cemetery transaction or interment. The notary completes a **jurat** to authenticate the witness's identity and sworn testimony.

PURPOSE: Records statements from witnesses regarding events, observations, or transactions related to cemetery property or operations.

CITATION: **La. C.E. art. 802 – Hearsay Exceptions; Statements of Witnesses**
"Statements made by witnesses with firsthand knowledge may be admissible when properly recorded and verified under oath."

DESCRIPTION: Used by cemetery management to preserve contemporaneous witness accounts, such as incidents, accidents, or ownership disputes, and filed with incident or case records for reference.

WITNESS STATEMENT FORM

STATE OF LOUISIANA
PARISH OF ______________________________

I, ____, a person of the age of majority, who after being duly sworn, state the following:

____

____

____

____

____

____

____

____

AFFIANT:

____
Signature of Affiant

____
Printed Name of Affiant

____
Date

SWORN TO AND SUBSCRIBED before me on
this ____ day of _______________, 20____

____
Signature of Notary

Printed Notary Name: _________________________________
Notary ID or Bar Roll No.: ________________
My Commission is for Life

FORM 6.3

DECLARATION OF DISPOSITION OF REMAINS

FORM: ✏ **NOTARIZATION REQUIRED**

FORM REQUIREMENTS: This instrument is a **sworn affidavit** and must be **subscribed and sworn before a Notary Public**. It serves as an evidentiary declaration under **La. C.C. art. 1836** and may be recorded in cemetery files or conveyance records for verification of burial authorization.
No witnesses are required.

PURPOSE: Allows a person to designate in writing who has authority to control the disposition of their remains.

CITATION: La. R.S. 8:655 – Right of Disposition; Written Directions
"A person may execute a written and notarized declaration designating the person or persons who shall have the right to control the disposition of his remains at death."

DESCRIPTION: Executed while living, this declaration governs who can authorize burial, cremation, or other final disposition. Filed with the cemetery or included with pre-need documentation.

DECLARATION OF DISPOSITION OF REMAINS

STATE OF LOUISIANA
PARISH OF ________________

BEFORE ME, the undersigned Notary Public, duly commissioned in and for the Parish of and state aforesaid, PERSONALLY, CAME AND APPEARED:

____________________________________, SSN xxx-xx-______a person of full age of majority, domiciled in ___________________ Parish, Louisiana, whose Date of Birth is__________________,

Who, after being duly sworn, did depose and state the following:

That he/she makes this declaration of disposition of his/her remains in accordance with the provisions of **La. R.S. 8:655 and 37:876**; that he/she is able to comprehend generally the nature of the actions which he is undertaking and voluntarily makes this declaration before the undersigned notary after a due reading of the whole; that he/she does hereby declare that upon his/her death that his/her body is to be cremated; that he/she does hereby declare that ______________________________ has authority over the disposition of his/her final remains, honor this request for disposition of his/her remains by cremation; and that he/she does hereby authorize and empower the funeral director, funeral home, and crematorium to accept this declaration as authority for cremation of his/her remains.

____
Signature of Affiant

________________________________, AFFIANT
Printed Name of Affiant

SWORN TO AND SUBSCRIBED before me on
this ____ day of ______________, 20____

____
Signature of Notary

Printed Notary Name: ___________________________
Notary ID or Bar Roll No.: ______________
My Commission is for Life

FORM 6.4

DECLARATION OF DISPOSITION OF REMAINS UNDER A MANDATE

FORM: ✐ **NOTARIZATION REQUIRED**

FORM REQUIREMENTS: This instrument is a **sworn affidavit** and must be **subscribed and sworn before a Notary Public**. It serves as an evidentiary declaration under **La. C.C. art. 1836** and may be recorded in cemetery files or conveyance records for verification of burial authorization.
No witnesses are required.

PURPOSE: Appoints a mandatary (agent) to exercise authority over burial or cremation decisions in accordance with Louisiana Civil Code provisions on mandates.

CITATION: La. C.C. art. 2989 – Nature of Mandate
"A mandate is a contract by which a person, the principal, confers authority on another person, the mandatary, to transact one or more affairs for the principal."

DESCRIPTION: Used to grant a trusted representative decision-making authority over disposition matters and recognized under both civil law and Title 8 when properly executed.

DECLARATION OF DISPOSITION OF REMAINS AUTHORIZED UNDER A MANDATE

STATE OF LOUISIANA
PARISH OF ________________

BEFORE ME, the undersigned Notary Public, duly commissioned in and for the Parish of aforesaid, PERSONALLY, CAME AND APPEARED:

_______________________________________, SSN xxx-xx-______a person of full age of majority, domiciled in ___________________ Parish, Louisiana, whose Date of Birth is_______________________, who did declare:

By virtue of the Power of Attorney I hold for _______________________ ____________, herein "Principal." I hereby declare that I make this notarized declaration of disposition of his/her remains in accordance with the provisions of **La. R.S. 8:655 and 37:876**; that I am of sound mind and voluntarily make this declaration before the undersigned Notary Public after a due reading of the whole; that I do hereby declare that upon the PRINCIPAL'S death, that his/her body be cremated. I do hereby authorize and empower the funeral director, funeral establishment, or crematory authority to accept this notarized declaration as authority for cremation of PRINCIPAL'S remains.

____
Signature of Affiant

________________________________, AFFIANT
Printed Name of Affiant

SWORN TO AND SUBSCRIBED before me on this ____ day of _____________, 20____

____
Signature of Notary

Printed Notary Name: ____________________________
Notary ID or Bar Roll No.: ______________
My Commission is for Life

Appendix

Miscellaneous Notarial Tools

SAMPLE CEMETERY ACCEPTANCE STAMP

The following can be used to create a stamp for documents to be accepted by the cemetery.

CONSENT OF CEMETERY AUTHORITY

The Cemetery Authority does hereby consent to this conveyance, subject to the reservations and conditions expressed herein, and hereby agrees to record such in its official records.

____

Cemetery Authority Authorized Representative

FORMS OF ACKNOWLEDGMENT

According to LA. R.S. 35:511

(Begin in all cases by a caption specifying the state and place where the acknowledgment is taken).

Type of Person	Statutory Form
Natural Persons Acting in Their Own Right	On this _______ day of ________, 20__, __________ before me personally appeared A B (or A B and C D), to me known to be the person (or persons) described in and who executed the foregoing instrument, and acknowledged that he (or they) executed it as his (or their) free act and deed.
Natural Persons Acting by Attorney	On this _______ day of _______, 20__, before me personally appeared A B, to me known to be the person who executed the foregoing instrument in behalf of C D, and acknowledged that he executed it as the free act and deed of said C D. (In all cases add signature and title of the officer taking the acknowledgment)
Corporations or Joint Stock Associations	On this ________ day of ________, 20__, before me appeared A B, to me personally known, who, being by me duly sworn (or affirmed) did say that he is the president (or other officer or agent of the corporation or association), of (describing the corporation or association), and that the seal affixed to said instrument is the corporate seal of said corporation (or association) and that the instrument was signed and sealed in behalf of the corporation (or association) by authority of its Board of Directors (or trustees) and that A B acknowledged the instrument to be the free act and deed of the corporation (or association). (In case the corporation or association has no corporate seal, omit the words "the seal affixed to said instrument is the corporate seal of the corporation (or association), and that" and add, at the end of the affidavit clause, the words "and that the corporation (or association) has no corporate seal")

PREAMBLE EXAMPLES

This list is not exhaustive, but rather a sampling of options for use by notaries.
when preparing a preamble/introduction clause.

Location	Example Clause
Within the notary's parish of Commission	BEFORE ME, the undersigned notary public, duly commissioned and qualified in and for the aforesaid state and parish, PERSONALLY CAME AND APPEARED
	BEFORE ME, JOHN H. DEAUX, duly commissioned and qualified in and for the state and parish aforesaid, and in the presence of the undersigned competent witnesses, Jane H. Deaux and James Deaux, PERSONALLY CAME AND APPEARED
Outside the notary's parish of commission, but in another parish where the notary is qualified	BEFORE ME, the undersigned notary public, duly commissioned in and for the Parish of Vermilion, and qualified statewide, PERSONALLY CAME AND APPEARED
	BEFORE ME, JOHN H. DEAUX, duly commissioned in and for the Parish of Vermilion, and qualified statewide and in the presence of the undersigned competent witnesses, Jane H. Deaux and James Deaux, PERSONALLY CAME AND APPEARED
	BEFORE ME, the undersigned notary public, duly commissioned in and for the Parish of Vermilion and qualified in the Parish of Iberia, PERSONALLY CAME AND APPEARED

MARITAL STATUS OF PARTIES

Whenever notaries pass any acts they shall give the marital status of all parties to the act, viz., if either or any party or parties are men, they shall be described as single, married, or widower. If married or widowed, the Christian and family name of the wife shall be given. If either or any party or parties are women, they shall be described as single, married or widow. If married or widow, their christian and family name shall be given, adding that she is the wife of or widow of... the husband's name." (**La. R.S. 35:11**)

Marital Status	Example
Party is currently single (whether never married or divorced but not remarried)	John H. Deaux…, a single man… Jane H. Deaux…, a single woman…
Party is currently married	John H. Deaux, married to Jane H. Deaux (neé Savoie) John H. Deaux, husband of Jane H. Deaux (neé Savoie) Jane H. Deaux, married to John H. Deaux Jane H. Deaux, wife of John H. Deaux
Party is currently married, but appearing together	Jane H. Deaux (neé Savoie) and John H. Deaux, husband and wife, appearing together.
Party is a widow or a widower but has not remarried	Jane H. Deaux, widow of John H. Deaux John H. Deaux, widower of Jane H. Deaux (neé Savoie)

MARITAL HISTORY OF PARTIES

Marital History	Example
Single and never married	John H. Deaux, declaring himself to be a single man, never having been married…
Divorced and not remarried	John H. Deaux, declaring himself to be a single man, having been married only once, and then to Jane H. Deaux (neé Savoie) from whom he is judicially divorced…
Widowed and not remarried	Jane H. Deaux (neé Savoie), declaring herself to be a widow, having been married only once and then to John H. Deaux, now deceased…
When a party has been married multiple times	John H. Deaux, declaring that he is a married man of the full age of majority domiciled in the Parish of Lafayette, State of Louisiana, and that his permanent mailing address is 123 Main St., Lafayette, LA 70501, and declaring further that he has been married three times, first to Jane M. Hudson, now deceased, whose death on September 13, 1984, in Kaplan, Louisiana, ended that marriage; then to Christine Adams, from whom he was divorced on April 1, 1992, by judgment of the 15th Judicial Court for the Parish of Lafayette, State of Louisiana; and then to Katharine Romero, with whom he is currently married…

Made in United States
North Haven, CT
11 November 2026

22097459R00157